Write it Better – A Study of Relevant Residential Report Writing

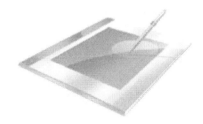

A Guide for the Written Residential Appraisal Report

First Edition March 2017

Written by

Diana T. Jacob

1Ed03-2017

Introduction

Since the advent of the Dodd Frank Act and implementation of the Uniform Appraisal Data (UAD) required communication in the mortgage lending world, the scrutiny of the narrative support for Residential Form reporting has been substantial. The regulations of the secondary markets known as assignment conditions (defined in the Uniform Standards of Professional Appraisal Practice i.e. USPAP and policies of secondary lending) have specific directives and admonitions. This course highlights core considerations of communicating key points in the residential appraisal assignment. The illustrative examples and collection and excerpts of Handbooks, Selling Guide, and the Uniform Standards of Professional Appraisal Practice (USPAP) are presented to enhance the skills of the participant interested in their performance of a residential appraisal assignment. This is a hands-on curriculum requiring interactive participation.

This educational publication was developed by Diana T. Jacob published by A Ladder Up Publishing and Texas Association of Appraisers, who shares the copyright privileges of those original contents and format of the contents. The reproduction of this publication in part or as a whole is strictly limited for those attendees/purchasers of this educational course offering. Any other publication is prohibited without first seeking the permission of the author. This text has been developed through extensive research of various sources, many of whom have been noted in the footnotes throughout the text. Clipart and graphics were reproduced from Microsoft clip art, and those offered which are not copyrighted on the website from various sources used in the research noted in the footnotes.   Various Logos shown are not an endorsement of any governmental agency nor private enterprise or educational organization for this course.

The text materials have been designed for the sole purpose of an educational enhancement and ***should not be construed*** as a legal opinion nor is it an authorization by various State Licensing and Certification Boards for Real Estate Appraisal in terms of their expectations. Nor should the content of the text or supplemental course materials be considered wholly in its content as a means for assuring compliance with all federal and state laws, USPAP or any entity and their Laws and Regulations. The users of this educational text are encouraged to seek professional legal advice when applying the knowledge of this course in any valuation service that carries a legal liability.

Diana T. Jacob

1Ed03-2017

About the Author

Diana Jacob currently lives in Lafayette, Louisiana, her childhood state and initial appraisal beginnings. She holds the certified general certification from the states of North Carolina and Texas and residential certification from the state of Louisiana. She is certified to teach the Uniform Standards of Professional Appraisal Practice (USPAP) by the Appraiser Qualifications Board (AQB) of The Appraisal Foundation. She aided in the original development of the 15-Hour USPAP Course mandated to be attended by all licensed and certified real estate appraisers. While serving on the original Ad Hoc Committee and later on the first Education Council of The Appraisal Foundation Sponsors (ECAFS), she drafted the operating procedures of ECAFS. She has taught a variety of appraisal courses through the U.S. for several schools and associations. She is well known as a prominent appraisal instructor and author, beginning with Financial Analysis of Income Producing Properties in 1990. She currently teaches both continuing education courses and has authored more than twenty-five formal publications including papers, course curriculum and texts. She has eight grandchildren ranging in ages from 1 through 22. Her hobbies are cooking, watching movies, gardening and playing with her dogs.

Table of Contents

Chapter 1

Chapter 2

Chapter 3

The Narrative Support for Results of the Sales Approach   **3-1**

Chapter 4

Other Approaches and Final Reconciliation   **4-1**

Chapter 5

Solutions to Case Study and Class Discussion Exercises   **5-1**

Supplemental Chapter   **Collective Comments**

Research Sources

FHA Website

2016-2017 Uniform Standards of Professional Appraisal Practice

Appendix D to HUD Handbook 4000.1,

Comments constructed by the author and shared in textbooks written by Diana T. Jacob

1Ed03-2017

Chapter 1

Relevant Communication of the Scope of Work

Chapter Objectives

- Recognizing the Pitfalls and Relevancy of Boiler Plate
- Review the Minimum Contents of USPAP Standard 2 in the Written Report
- Identify minimum requirements of communicating the results of a Contract Analysis

1.1   Boiler Plate Communication

Appraising residential properties successfully as a business means production over a short period. The ability to communicate sufficiently for the intended user and in compliance with the multi layers of regulations gives certainty that some "boiler plating" verbiage benefits the intended user and the author. The critical step in knowing when "boiler plating" is necessary is to first identify whether its relevant to the understanding and compliance of the appraisal report.

The boiler plate offers informative snapshots. For example; "The lack of close proximity to major shopping centers and public transportation is not an adverse factor in this rural location. The appeal of this rural location is centered on quiet enjoyment, lax governmental regulations on land use and proximity distance to nearest urban market being approximately 30 minutes driving distance (under 40 miles)."

Exercise 1
What are three things you learned from the "boilerplate" example?

_____

_____

_____

1.1.1   Boilerplating

There are certain statements that may be requested within the body of your report that will require for example statements in addition to the form:

USPAP	State Law	Underwriter Guidelines	[1]Investor Overlays
Exposure Time	Fee Disclosure	Utilities Turned On	Value over Predominant Price
History of Service	Smoke Alarms	FHA 10% line, 15% net, and 25% gross adjustment	PUD common elements even when builder is not in control
Source of Market Value Definition	Carbon Monoxide Detectors	Interior Photographs	Details of "Other" Land Use
Disclosure of potential Impact when using Hypothetical Conditions or Extraordinary Assumptions	Fees that were paid to the appraiser	Calculations proving Gross Living Area (GLA)	
Who may have provided significant assistance	Fees that were charged by the AMC	Who is in control of HOA	
		Who is responsible for private street maintenance	

Developing a statement or sentence with blank lines in a template format can increase the strength of compliance when writing the report.

Example: "The subject is "proposed or under construction", as such the appraiser has been asked to condition this market value opinion under the "specific assumption" that the improvements have been completed in a workman like manner. It must be understood this is a known false condition; if the improvements are not completed as scheduled the results of this appraisal may be impacted."

---

[1] A specific policy such as when a lender requires PUD data be completed even though the builder is not in control

1.2 Minimal Reporting Requirements of USPAP

Consider the following items that USPAP exhorts a written Appraisal Report to contain.

²USPAP List of Reporting Requirements			
Location in Document	STD 1 Development	Reporting Descriptor	Basic Content
Ethics Rule Conduct		SUMMARIZE	Line 247-251 - .."an appraiser must disclose to the client, and in each subsequent report certification: any current or prospective interest in the subject property or parties involved; and ANY services regarding the subject property performed by the appraiser within the three-year period immediately preceding acceptance of the assignment, as an appraiser or in any other capacity."....
Ethics Rule Management		SUMMARIZE	Line 260-265.."must disclose that he or she paid a fee or commission, or gave a thing of value in connection with procurement of an assignment. Disclosure must appear in the certification AND in any transmittal letter in which conclusions are stated; ...disclosure of the amount paid in not required."..
Ethics Rule Confidentiality			Line 289-296 ...MUST NOT disclose (1) confidential information; or (2) assignment results to anyone other than: <ul><li>the client;</li><li>parties specifically authorized by the client;</li><li>State appraiser regulatory agencies;</li><li>Third parties authorized by due process of law; or</li><li>Peer review committee (exception when disclosure would violate law or regulation</li></ul>
Competency Rule		DESCRIBE	Describe lack of knowledge and/or experience plus steps taken and acknowledgment of this disclosure was made to the client prior to the completion of the assignment and approved.

---

² 2016-2017 Edition Of USPAP

\[3\]USPAP List of Reporting Requirements			
Location in Document	STD 1 Development	Reporting Descriptor	Basic Content
Scope of Work		SUMMARIZE	Line 452 "..report must contain sufficient information to allow intended users to understand the scope of work performed....Sufficient information includes disclosure of research and analyses performed and might also include disclosure of research and analyses not performed.
Jurisdictional Exception Rule			Lines 462 ..."4) cite in the report the law or regulation requirement this exception to USPAP compliance.
STD 2			Each analysis, opinion, and conclusion must be reported in a manner that is NOT misleading.
SR 2-1 (a), (b), (c)		MUST	Clearly and accurately communicate in manner not misleading, contain sufficient information to enable the intended users of the appraisal to understand; and clearly and accurately disclose all assumptions, extraordinary assumptions, hypothetical conditions, and limiting conditions used in the assignment.
SR 2-2		Prominently State	Report Option, Appraisal Report or Restricted Appraisal Report
SR 2-2(a)		MUST BE Consistent	With Intended Use
SR 2-2(a) (i)	1-2(a)	STATE	Identity of the client
SR 2-2(a) (ii)	1-2(b)	STATE	The intended use of appraiser's opinions and conclusions

\[3\] 2016-2017 Edition Of USPAP

⁴USPAP List of Reporting Requirements			
Location in Document	**STD 1 Development**	**Reporting Descriptor**	**Basic Content**
SR 2-2 (a) (iii)	1-2 (e)	SUMMARIZE	Information SUFFICIENT to identify the real estate involved, including physical, legal, and economic property characteristics relevant to the assignment
SR 2-2 (a) (iv)	1-2-(e)(ii)	STATE	Real property interest
SR 2-2 (a) (v)	1-2(c)	STATE	Type of Value
SR 2-2 (a) (v)		STATE	Definition of Value
SR 2-2 (a) (v)		Cite Source	Definition of Value
SR 2-2 (a) (v)	1-(2) (c) (iv)		If Market Value; state if (1) cash or equivalent, or (2) based on non-market
SR 2-2 (a) (v)	1-(2) (c) (iv)	STATE	Exposure time (if Mkt Value) must be reported
SR 2-2 (a) (vi)	1-2 (d) Effective Date only	STATE	Effective date of the appraisal AND the report
SR 2-2 (a) (vii)	1-2 (h)	SUMMARIZE	Scope of work used to develop the appraisal; includes disclosure of research and analyses performed and MIGHT ALSO include disclosure of research and analyses NOT PERFORMED
SR 2-2 (a) (xi)	1-2 (f) and (g)	STATE	Clearly and conspicuously all extraordinary assumptions and hypothetical conditions
SR 2-2 (a) (xi)		STATE	That their use might have affected the assignment results
SR 2-2 (a) (viii)	SR 1-2(h) Determine SOW necessary to produce credible results	SUMMARIZE	Information analyzed, appraisal methods and techniques employed, and the reasoning that supports the analyses, opinions, and conclusions
SR 2-2 (viii)	SR 1-4 (a),(b),(c)	SUMMARIZE	Exclusion of any one of the three approaches to value MUST BE EXPLAINED

\(^5\)USPAP List of Reporting Requirements			
Location in Document	**STD 1 Development**	**Reporting Descriptor**	**Basic Content**
SR 2-2 (a) (viii)	SR 1-4 (a), (b), (c)	SUMMARIZE	MUST provide sufficient information to enable client and intended users to understand rationale for the opinions and conclusions, including reconciliation of the data and approaches, in accordance with SR 1-6
SR 2-2 (a) (viii)	SR 1-5	SUMMARIZE	MUST provide a summary of the results of analyzing the Subject Sales, Agreements of Sale, Options, and Listings in Accordance with SR 1-5. If information is unavailable, MUST provide a statement on efforts undertaken to obtain information. If information is irrelevant, MUST provide a statement on existence of information AND CITE its lack of relevance
SR 2-2 (a) (ix)	SR 1-3 (a) MUST in Mkt. V. identify AND analyze effect on use AND value of existing land use regulations, reasonably probable modifications of land use regulations, economic supply and demand, physical adaptability of the real estate AND market trends. MUST AVOID unsupported conclusions about mkt trends, effective age and remaining life.	STATE	Use of the real estate existing as of the date of value AND the use of the real estate reflected in the appraisal

\(^5\) 2016-2017 Edition of USPAP

[6]USPAP List of Reporting Requirements			
Location in Document	**STD 1 Development**	**Reporting Descriptor**	**Basic Content**
SR 2-2 (a) (x)	SR 1-3 (b) An appraiser MUST analyze the relevant legal, physical, and economic factors to the extent necessary to support the appraiser's highest and best use conclusions.	SUMMARIZE	When an opinion of Highest and Best Use was developed, SUMMARIZE the support AND Rationale for that opinion.
SR 2-2(a) (xii)	Ethics Rule	INCLUDE	Signed certification in accordance with SR 2-3

[6] 2016-2017 Edition of USPAP contact The Appraisal Foundation www.appraisalfoundation.org for a complete copy

1.3   Scope of Work - Contract Analysis

When the appraiser has been engaged because of a pending sale part of the appraisal assignment will involve a contract analysis. In the Uniform Standards of Professional Appraisal Practice, (USPAP), the development rule of a real property appraisal Standard Rule (SR), 1-5 demands the analysis of a contract. One of the more common errors that appraisers make is their failure to actually read the contract due to its length and legal verbiage that seems non-relevant to the appraiser's task in the assignment.

C O N T R A C T	I ☐ did ☐ did not analyze the contract for sale for the subject purchase transaction. Explain the results of the analysis of the contract for sale or why the analysis was not performed.
	Contract Price $ Date of Contract Is the property seller the owner of public record? ☐Yes ☐No Data Source(s)
	Is there any financial assistance (loan charges, sale concessions, gift or downpayment assistance, etc.) to be paid by any party on behalf of the borrower? ☐ Yes ☐ No If Yes, report the total dollar amount and describe the items to be paid.

Discussion Question(s):   1. Why is the contract pending relevant to the appraisal assignment?

2. Why is the history of the past three years relevant to the appraisal assignment?

What should an appraiser communicate in a contract analysis? The answer to this question begins with an overview of the form. There are basic questions that will need an answer.

1.3.1 Discussion Question(s)

1. **Did you receive the contract?** The first questions on the URAR form ask for the results or the reason the analysis was not performed.

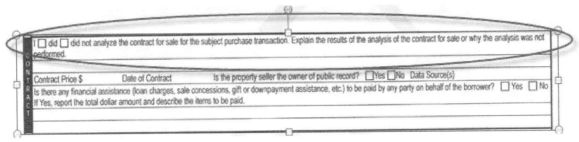

USPAP is very clear in the communication Standard Rule about minimum content of communication. Note the except from SR 2-2(a)(viii) in the comment section:

[7]*"Comment: An appraiser must maintain a specific, coherent workfile in support of a Restricted Appraisal Report. The contents of the workfile must include sufficient information to indicate that the appraiser complied with the requirements of STANDARD 1 and for the appraiser to produce an Appraisal Report.*

When reporting an opinion of market value, a summary of the results of analyzing the subject sales, agreements of sale, options, and listings in accordance with Standards Rule 1-5 is required. If such information is unobtainable, a statement on the efforts undertaken by the appraiser to obtain the information is required. If such information is irrelevant, a statement acknowledging the existence of the information and citing its lack of relevance is required."

Notice there are three directives of communication:
1. There must be a summary of the results of analyzing the SUBJECT sales, agreements of sale, options, and listings in accordance with SR 1-5, and
2. If such information is unobtainable, a statement on the efforts undertaken by the appraiser to obtain the information is required.
3. If such information is irrelevant, a statement acknowledging the existence of the information and citing its lack of relevance is required.

It's one thing to analyze the sales agreement, most appraisers will take a "shot" at reading the basic terms and conditions but what about the listing of the subject? What about the prior sales of the Subject? Did you ask if there were any "options"? Not all real estate purchases involve an immediate sale. There is also a contract known as an "option contract". It's a contract NOT TO REVOKE an offer once it's made. It can also be used to bring about the sale of real estate, but on a very different schedule than usual. The thought behind this type of

---

[7] Excerpt from 2016-2017 Edition of USPAP, page 26, in commentary of SWR 2-2(a) (viii); go to www.appraisalfoundation.org for full understanding of the communication requirements when analyzing a contract for a sale pending.

contract is the homeowner can extend and keep open an offer to sell, in return for compensation by the buyer (known as the "optionee"). That offer will remain open for a specific period of time, at a certain price, and to a specific potential buyer. In many cases the buyer is a tenant, currently renting the property and thereby creating what is called a "lease-option contract". Another example could be a developer who is interested in a specific plot of land but needs to have time to do more research and obtain permits before any commitment to the purchase can be made. When an option is exercised in accordance to the defined terms and conditions the option becomes a binding contract. The seller must sell, and the buyer must buy, for the stipulated price or legal consideration stated in the option. That exercised option is now a binding contract with the stated terms and conditions reiterated in the executory contract (one that is in process of being completed, i.e. there is a transfer of the title).

In an option contract only the seller is legally bound (the buyer is not). It's a benefit to the seller in that they may be in a market that is over-supplied and slow moving; this commitment has a consideration so the time the property is taken off of the market the seller is compensated (usually by a monthly rental payment). For the buyer, the benefit is additional time to gather the downpayment, clean up their credit, and have inspections completed for assurance of conditions. The option is also seen in some cases as an investment. When a third party buys the option, they are buying the property at the terms of the option, waiting for a realized increase (anticipated at the time of the option purchase). They are also waiting for a potential profit if they find a buyer who wants to pay more than the cost of the property bound by the seller to sell.

Your analysis of a current option would include the communication that there is a known encumbrance to the "Fee Simple" estate because the seller has already committed to sell the property to a specific buyer for a stipulated amount.

It's important to understand that a contract written with a contingency (an exception to the sale agreement based on the occurrence of a certain event such as a sale of an existing home), is not an option. That is a sales contract with a contingency. An option to purchase would not contain that type of language. As stated, an option is not binding on the buyer until the buyer exercises their legal privilege to exercise the option. For an option to be considered "valid" there must be "consideration" to be legally enforceable, it must be in writing and be signed, by the seller. Although it is preferred to be signed by both buyer and seller, the signature of the seller is legally binding.

When analyzing your contract, a tool that can benefit that process is a grid that lays out the terms of the subject's contract (see subsequent page).

1.3.2 Development Grid to Identify Terms and Conditions of Contract

Sample Grid to Identify and Analyze the Terms of the Contract

Date of Analysis		Client Name/File No.		Analyst Name:
ITEM	Subject Property	Comparable No. 1	Comparable No. 2	Comparable No. 3
ADDRESS	DESCRIPTION	DESCRIPTION	DESCRIPTION	DESCRIPTION
Transaction Type (Cv, FHA, VA, Other)				
Loan to Value Ratio (LTV)				
Adjustable Rate, Fixed Rate, Assump. Interest (A.P.R.)				
Loan Term and Amortization Payments (i.e. 30 yr.'s monthly pmt.'s)				
Buy-Down Rate				
Buy-Down Terms				
Buy-Down Points				
Discount Points Paid by Seller				
Points Paid by Buyer				
Other Buyer Fees				
Other Seller Fees				
Personal Property				
Other Term(s)				
Source of Information				
Similar/Dissimilar				

1.3.3 Practice Development Grid -Identifying Terms and Conditions of Contract

Consider the following terms of the Subject's Contract. Review the completed information provided on hypothetical sales below and communicate a narrative commentary on the results of your contract analysis.

Subject Contract – Sale Pending $350,000 with no sales concessions, Refrigerator conveys, Conventional Loan, $70,000 Down-Payment seeking interest rate of 3.75% over 30 years, Fixed Rate of Interest

Item	Comp. #1	Comp. #2	Comp. #3	Comp. #4	Comp. #5
Address/MLS #	1321 Boering Dr NAVICA#184772	132 Trelawney NAVICA #180359	443 Laguna Vis NAVICA 183344	864 Shadylon Ln NAVICA#184094	4621 Shadylon Ln NAVICA#174594
Sale Price	$390,000	$260,000	$287,500	$600,000	$425,000
List Price	$410,500	$268,000	$270,300	$582,000	$482,000
Days on Market	141	241	350	158	158
Type of Transaction	Conventional	VA	FHA	Conventional	Conventional
Seller Paid Financial Concession	None	$11,700	$17,250	$32,400	None
Sales Concession	Refrigerator Exterior Kit Area Appliances & TV		All Free-Standing Appliances W/D, Refrigerator	Riding Lawnmower Refrigerator	Riding Lawnmower Refrigerator
Loan to Value Ratio	80/20	100%	90%	85/15	80/20
APR	3.5%	3.75%	4.2%	3.5%	3.67%

Additional Market Sales Data Pulled

Total Sales Considered Comparable ___20___ Sales Concessions

Personal Property

Personal Property

___8___ Sales pass with personal property no

___2___ Sales pass with concessions no

___10___ Sales pass with no concessions no

1.3.3.1 Practice Exercise

Based on the preceding page:

1. What is the dominant transaction type (dominant type of financing)?

   _____

2. Is there a trend that can be identified on concessions?

   _____

3. Is it customary for personal property to pass with the sale?

   _____

1.3.3.2 Writing Exercise

Based on your assignment results, write a narrative comment conveying to your client, a lender, the results of your contract analysis. Prior to writing, review the USPAP SR 2-2 (a) and SR 1-5 within this chapter (page 1-8) to guide your comments.

_____
_____
_____
_____
_____
_____

1.3.3.3 Using a Qualified Analysis Technique for Contract Analysis

One technique to assist in your decision-making is to use a comparison rating method. Consider the subject has a pending contract of $310,000, is seeking conventional financing with a Sale to List Price Ratio of 97% based on a list price of $310,000. The seller has conceded to a maximum of $15,000 to be paid toward financing costs. You have selected the group of sales you believe are most similar to the subject with the following reported details of their financing terms:

Item	Comp. #1	Comp. #2	Comp. #3	Comp. #4	Comp. #5
Address/MLS #	NAVICA #184772	NAVICA #180359	NAVICA #183344	NAVICA #184094	NAVICA #174594
Sale Price	$390,000	$260,000	$287,500	$600,000	$425,000
List Price	$410,500	$268,000	$270,300	$582,000	$482,000
Sale to List Ratio	0.950060901	0.970149254	1.063633	1.030927835	0.881742739
Days on Market	141	241	350	158	158
Type of Financing	Conventional	VA	FHA	Conventional	Conventional
Seller Paid Financial Concession	0	$11,700	$17,250	$32,400	$0
Percent Seller Pd Concession to SP	0.00%	4.50%	6.00%	5.40%	0.00%
Loan to Value Ratio	80%	100%	90%	85%	80%
APR	3.50%	3.50%	4.20%	3.50%	3.67%

The greater number of sales the lower degree of margin of error. For the purpose of this exercise consider the five sales above and draw conclusions based on the median conclusion:

Results of Analysis			
Sale to List Ratio Median	0.970149254		
Seller Paid Concessions Median	11700		
Percent of Concessions to Sale Price Median	4.50%		
Days on the Market Median	158		
Dominant Type of Financing	Conventional		
Range of Comparable Sale Prices	$268,000 - $315,000		
Predominant Sale Price	$390,000	median	
Predominant List Price	$270,000	(rounded to nearest thousand)	

Using the results of your analysis compare those conclusions to the subject's pending contract.

Results of Analysis			
Sale to List Ratio Median	0.970149254		
Seller Paid Concessions Median	11700		
Percent of Concessions to Sale Price Median	4.50%		
Days on the Market Median	158		
Dominant Type of Financing	Conventional		
Range of Comparable Sale Prices	$268,000 - $315,000		
Predominant Sale Price	$390,000	median	
Predominant List Price	$270,000	(rounded to nearest thousand)	

Using a scale of 1-5 (1 being low and 5 being the most similar or equal to), rate the subject's pending contract to the analysis results.

Subject Contract Comparison to Market		Rating	Scale 1-5 low to high		
Sale Price	$310,000	3			
Financing	Conventional	5			
List Price	$319,600	5			
Sale to List Price Raio	0.969962453	5			
Seller Paid Concessions	$15,000	4			
Percent of Concessions to Sale Price	0.048387097	4			
		26	30 Points Strong Performance with Market		
			25 Points Good Performance with Market		
			20 Points Average Performance in the Market		
			15 Points Not in line with typical market behavior		

1.4   Additional examples when reporting contract analysis results

When you read through various secondary market publications and resources, one of the recommendations that are made is that the appraiser notes the number of pages in the contract they received. Some publications request a statement made as to the enforceability of the contract. The appraiser must keep in mind and ensure the reader recognizes the limitations of the appraiser when reviewing contracts.

Sample Contract Supplemental Comment-(This comment would be in the addendum as it will not fit into the space offered on the form)

Sample 1) Explain the results (on the form): The executory contract (one which is signed by both parties) included in the $_____ sale price a seller agreement to pay up to $_____ towards closing costs and to leave the refrigerator and custom curtains in the living room. These contingencies are within the normal negotiations (terms of a sale) between buyers and sellers of similar properties in this market.

Sample 2) When only one signature (buyer) was included
Explain the results (on the form): The voidable contract (one which is signed by the buyer only) included in the $_____ sale price a seller agreement to pay up to $_____ towards closing costs and leave the refrigerator and custom curtains in the living room. If the seller agrees to these terms these contingencies are within the normal negotiations (terms of a sale) between buyers and sellers of similar properties in this market.

However, without the seller's signature, the appraiser makes it known this contract is not binding nor is it considered a valid enforceable contract.

1.5 Sale Price changes or Renegotiations after the Report Delivery

Much confusion and frustration arises from sale prices that are changed due to renegotiations after the appraisal has been turned in. Points to consider in this situation are:

- Any current sale pending analysis by the appraiser was written prior to the effective date of the appraisal and may be one that is not based on one or both parties having knowledge or being well-informed.

- Any subsequent renegotiated contract occurs after the appraisal with buyers and sellers having new information making their sale price an informed condition of their exchange.

- The secondary market issued an announcement to lenders about contract amendments and the issue of requiring an appraisal report to be revised as a result of that amended contract.

[8]Q7. Why does Fannie Mae require the lender to provide the sales contract to the appraiser? Response: Fannie Mae's policy is intended to help ensure that the appraiser is aware of all relevant aspects of the transaction. The sales contract provides important sales and financing data, including whether there are any concessions as part of the transaction. *__If the contract is amended__*, the lender must provide the updated contract to the appraiser to ensure that the appraiser has been given the opportunity to consider any changes and their effect on value. If the appraiser determines that there is no impact to value, then no additional commentary is required from the appraiser.

- An appraiser's analysis is a confirmation to the client/intended user that the contract either reflects market terms or it doesn't. That information is necessary to the client when making decisions about how they can approach financing terms (higher LTV, higher interest rate, etc.).

---

[8] February 12, 2016 Fannie Mae FAQ

- A renegotiation of a sale price doesn't change the value or impact the value or the marketability or any part of the valuation process. What it does change is the appraiser's comments on how the renegotiated price either does or does not have similarity of the market terms identified by the appraiser during the appraisal process in the market analysis of the neighborhood.

[9]FAQ Guidance from the Appraiser Standards Board on the request
137. DOES CHANGING THE SALE PRICE RESULT IN A NEW ASSIGNMENT?

Question: I recently completed an appraisal for mortgage financing purposes in a purchase transaction and delivered the report to my client. My opinion of value did not support the pending sale price. As a result, the purchase transaction was not consummated. However, one week later the buyer and seller entered into a new purchase agreement where the sale price coincided with my appraised value. My client asked if I can provide a revised report that includes the analysis of the newly agreed-upon sale price. To provide a revised appraisal report, must I consider the client's request as a new assignment?

Response: If the client does not require a more current effective date, USPAP *would not mandate treating the request as a new assignment*. However, if the client does require a more current effective date, the request must be treated as a new assignment. *In this example, regardless of whether the effective date is changed, the date of the report would have to change to accurately reflect the appraiser's consideration of the newly obtained agreement of sale.* Because the new purchase agreement was obtained *after* the date of the first report, the revised report would need to have a date of report that is the same as or later than the date the new purchase agreement was obtained by the appraiser.

Definition of Assignment, **Valuation Service and Value– According to USPAP (2016-2017 edition)**

ASSIGNMENT: 1) An agreement between an appraiser and a client to provide a valuation service; 2) the valuation service that is provided as a consequence of such an agreement.

VALUATION SERVICES: services pertaining to aspects of property value. **Comment:** Valuation services pertain to all aspects of property value and include services performed both by appraisers and by others.

VALUE: the monetary relationship between properties and those who buy, sell, or use those properties.

Comment: *Value* expresses an economic concept. As such, it is never a fact but always an opinion of the worth of a property at a given time in accordance with a specific definition of value. In appraisal practice, value must always be qualified - for example, market value, liquidation value, or investment value.

---

[9] Excerpted from the 2016-2017 edition of USPAP published by The Appraisal Foundation. For a current copy go to www.appraisalfoundation.org to order and to read and confer the excerpt cited on this page

In addition, the new report would also need to reflect the appraiser's analysis of the prior agreement of sale. In the development of an appraisal, an appraiser is required under Standards Rule 1-1(b), to *not commit a substantial error of omission or commission that significantly affects an appraisal*. Since information about the prior agreement of sale is known by the appraiser and that information is relevant to the appraisal problem, it must be considered.

Making the Decision-New Assignment?

To help make the decision as to whether or not the renegotiated sale it is a new assignment one needs to consider "is the pending sale or renegotiated sale price a value?". According to USPAP definition a value is never a fact. A sale price offer, acceptance or offer and acceptance states a price which once stated is a fact. In some cases state appraisal boards have "dinged" appraisers for failing to treat the renegotiated sale price as a new assignment. State rules and regulations would need to be followed as state laws, rules and regulations can exceed USPAP.

A renegotiated sale price is not a new appraisal but it may be considered a new assignment under some state laws. To ensure understanding on the intended user's behalf you must be sure to communicate in the report the reason why the value effective date may be so significantly different from the report date. A history of what transpired between the first report date and the second report date is in order.

Sample 3) Comment:

The appraiser informs the reader that any subsequent valid or voidable contract requested to be analyzed beyond this report date will not be considered an extension of this assignment. Rather it will be considered an amendment to the assignment but will require additional analysis, comments and a new report date thus such additional work will be subject to additional charges. In the event the request is agreed to by the appraiser the intended users must also accept that history of the first pending sale will be identified in the subsequent report.

Sample 4) Comment:

The appraiser informs the client the renegotiated sale price, after the effective date of the appraisal, does not affect the value conclusion on the effective date. The terms of a lowered sale price and amended concessions are not relevant to the value as of the effective date.

Additional Comments on a Supplemental Addendum

Comments on Contract Analysis: "The contract (found in the appraiser's workfile/attached as an exhibit) was believed to be the final ratified contract including all addendums and final accepted counter offers. This contract included __9__ pages. In the event a new contract was written after the effective date of this appraisal or subsequent to the receipt of the contract analyzed by the appraiser, the appraiser makes it known that it was not part of this assignment analysis.

The inclusion of personal property in the contract, i.e. washer, refrigerator, was deemed by the appraiser to be a concession of the sale. This personal property was not considered in the final value conclusion of the real property interest. Further the appraiser makes it known that he or she ***did not inspect the personal property*** nor does the appraiser warrant its functional utility. The items of personal property do not, in the appraiser's opinion, impact the sale price upward or downward but are seen as a typical concession between buyers and sellers in virtually all transactions. The lack of these items would not, in the appraiser's opinion, prevent the sale from passing or affect the price that was negotiated between the parties."

Chapter 2

Conveying the Connection-Neighborhood Analysis to the Highest and Best Use

Chapter Objectives

- Identifying Characteristics of a Neighborhood
- Review factors of a Trend Analysis
- Connect the Neighborhood Analysis to the Highest and Best Use of the Subject

> **Neighborhood**: A **residential** area is a land use in which housing predominates, as opposed to industrial and commercial areas. Housing may vary significantly between, and through, **residential** areas. These include single-family housing, multi-family **residential**, or mobile homes.
>
> Definition from "Residential Area-Wikipedia
> https://en.wikipedia.org/wiki/Residential_area

2.1 Regulating Authorities Perspective

Residential valuation begins with the recognition of the location, the identification of the greatest impact, the characteristics of the neighborhood. Viewing the neighborhood from the regulating authorities perspective gives the appraiser greater insight into what needs to be considered and communicated in the written Appraisal Report.

Fannie Mae says, *"[1]Neighborhood characteristics and trends influence the value of one- to four-unit residences. Therefore, an analysis of the subject property's neighborhood is a key element in the appraisal process. As a reminder, Fannie Mae purchases mortgages secured by properties in all neighborhoods and in all areas, as long as the property is acceptable as security for the mortgage based on its value and marketability.*

Neighborhood characteristics. These can be addressed by the types of structures (detached, attached) and architectural styles in the neighborhood (such as row or townhouse, colonial, ranch, or Victorian); current land use (such as single-family residential, commercial, or industrial); typical site size (such as 10000 sf or 2.00 ac); or street patterns or design (such as one-way street, cul-de-sac, or court).
The appraiser must fully consider all of the value-influencing characteristics in the neighborhood and arrive at an appropriate neighborhood description and opinion of value for the property, even if this requires more extensive research for particular property types or for properties in certain geographic locations.
In performing a neighborhood analysis, the appraiser
- *collects pertinent data,*
- *conducts a visual inspection of the neighborhood to observe its physical characteristics and determine its boundaries, and*
- *identifies land uses and any signs that the land uses are changing.*

---

[1] Excerpt from Fannie Mae Guidelines B4-1.3-03 Neighborhood Section of the Appraisal Report (9/30/2014)

VA Regulations – Pamphlet 26-7, Chapter 11, Item 8. Other Market Analysis Considerations

a. Introduction

The following market analysis considerations are provided as a reminder of VA appraisal expectations and as an aid in development of the appraisal report. Reporting each consideration, separate from the requirements of the appraisal report form is optional, unless time adjustments are used in the report.

b. Sales or Financing Concessions

The appraiser should report:

- *in the "Neighborhood" section of the Uniform Residential Appraisal Report (URAR) or on an addendum, the prevalence of sales or financing concessions (for example, interest rate buy-downs, inclusion of non-realty items in the transaction, seller payment of any buyer closing costs, etc.); and*
- *if any comparable sale involved concessions, the effect of the concessions on the sales price of the comparable should be noted. In doing so, the appraiser should consider:*
  - *that the effect of financing/sales concessions can vary in different locales,*
  - *that the amount of any adjustment should generally be based upon the real estate market reaction to the concession, and not on the dollar-for-dollar cost of the concession(s) to the seller, and*
  - *in proposed construction cases, closed sales by the same builder, sales in competitive subdivisions, and re-sales of similar existing properties.*

c. Housing Supply and Demand

In every case, the appraiser should:

- *consider the supply and demand for available housing in the subject market area, and*
- *report, either in the "Neighborhood" section of the URAR or on an addendum, the average listing price to sale price ratio for the subject market area. Professional judgment must be used to estimate that ratio if it cannot be determined from available data sources.*

d. Marketing Time and Trend

In every case, the appraiser should:

- *consider the marketing time trend (increasing or decreasing) in the subject market area, and*
- *report, either in the "Neighborhood" section of the URAR or on an addendum, the extent of increase or decrease in the average marketing time (listing period) in that market area. For example, "In the last 3 months, the listing period in the subject's market area decreased from 180 to 90 days."*

e. Sales Listings and Contract Offers	In every case, the appraiser should:

- *Analyze sales listings, contract offers, and unsettled sales to determine if market conditions changed between the date each comparable sold and the date of the subject property appraisal. This is especially important in markets with rapidly increasing or decreasing values. If the subject property is in a new subdivision, the analysis should include the builder's closed sales, sales in competitive subdivisions, and sales of similar existing properties.*
- *Certify, either in the "Neighborhood" section of the URAR or on an addendum: "I have considered relevant competitive listings/contract offerings in performing this appraisal, and any trend indicated by that data is supported by the listing/offering information included in this report."*
- *Provide a listings/offers addendum if a significant market transition is indicated in the "Neighborhood" section due to changes in employment opportunity, housing supply/demand, average marketing time, seller concessions, etc.*

Item 10   Remaining Economic Life

c. What the Appraiser Must Consider	*In estimating remaining economic life, the appraiser must consider:*

- *the relationship between the property and the economic stability of the block, neighborhood, and community;*
- *comparisons with homes in the same or similar areas;*
- *the need for a home of the particular type being appraised;*
- *the architectural design, style and utility from a functional point of view;*
- *the workmanship and durability of the construction, its physical condition, and probable cost of maintenance and/or repair;*
- *the extent to which other homes in the area are kept in repair; and*
- *in areas where rehabilitation and code enforcement are operating or under consideration, their expected results in improving the neighborhood for residential use.*

[2]FHA States, "b. Required Analysis and Reporting

The Appraiser must analyze the broad market area first (neighborhood analysis), then analyze the specific market (direct sales comparison), and then report how the subject relates to its market area.

The Appraiser must provide support for conclusions regarding housing trends and overall market conditions as reported in the "Neighborhood" section of the appraisal report form. The Appraiser's analysis and conclusions must be based on the information reported on this form. The Appraiser's study of the market affecting the subject Property must include sufficient data for a statistical analysis to be relevant.

---

[2] Page 556 HUD Handbook 4000.1

The Appraiser must fill in all the information to the extent it is available and reliable and must provide analysis as indicated. If any required data is unavailable or is considered unreliable, the Appraiser must provide an explanation. It is recognized that not all data sources will be able to provide data for the shaded areas on the form; if it is available, however, the Appraiser must include the data in the analysis.

If data sources provide the required information as an average instead of the median, the Appraiser must report the available figure and identify it as an average. The Appraiser must explain any anomalies in the data, such as seasonal markets, New Construction, foreclosures, etc.

Page 9 FHA Appraisal Report and Data Delivery Guide

3. Neighborhood Section

This section reflects the area surrounding the subject property. The appraiser must observe neighborhood characteristics and surrounding properties to make determinations that will be incorporated into the valuation of the subject property. In all instances, the appraiser must mark the appropriate box for each line in the "Neighborhood Characteristics" and "Housing Trends" sections. Failure to note conditions that may adversely affect the value of the property is poor appraisal practice and violates the Uniform Standards of Professional Appraisal Practice (USPAP).

The following table provides instruction for completing the "Neighborhood" section of the form. NOTE: Race and the racial composition of the neighborhood are not appraisal factors.

Field	Protocol

Location	• Enter the type of area surrounding the subject property:
	   o urban – relates to a city
	   o suburban – relates to an area adjacent to a city
	   o rural – relates to the country or beyond the suburban area
	   o Mark only one box that best describes the type of area.

Built-Up	• Enter the built-up percentage – the percentage of available land that has been improved. • Land such as a state park would not be considered available land.
Growth	• Enter the growth rate. • If many lots are available, the growth rate may be rapid, stable or slow, but if the neighborhood is fully developed, select the "Stable" box.

The following table provides instruction for completing the "One-Unit Housing Trends" section of the report form.

Field	Protocol
Property Values	• Mark the box describing the current trend in the As-Is Property Values for one-unit houses in the community. • Comparing houses that have been sold and resold in recent years is an effective way to determine market trends. • Appraisers who use this method, however, should make sure to factor in any improvements or changes made to the property between sales.
Supply	• To determine the equilibrium status of supply and demand in the neighborhood, compare the number of houses sold to the number of houses listed for sale in a recent time period. • The similarity or difference between the number of houses sold and listed, not the absolute numbers, should determine the demand/supply level.
Marketing Time	• Mark the appropriate marketing time – the typical length of time a one-unit property in the subject's neighborhood would have to stay on the market before being sold at a price near its Market Value.

The following table provides instruction for completing the "Present Land Use %" section of the report form.

Field	Protocol
Present Land Use %	• Estimate each type of land usage in the neighborhood. • If there is no land in the neighborhood with one of the designated classifications, enter 0. • If a portion of the land consists of parks or other unspecified classifications, enter the estimated percentages on the "Other" line and explain in the "Neighborhood Description" section. • Total of all land use must = 100%.

The following table provides instruction for completing the narrative "Neighborhood

Field	Protocol
Neighborhood Boundaries	• The appraiser must clearly define the boundaries – north, south, east and west – of the subject's neighborhood. • Provide a description of neighborhood boundaries by physical features (such as streets, rail lines, other man-made barriers or well-defined natural barriers, i.e. rivers, lakes, etc.), and details regarding neighborhood composition.

Neighborhood Description	• Discuss factors that would attract residents or cause them to reject the neighborhood. Some typical factors important to discuss include:
	  o level of maintenance and condition of housing
	  o housing styles, ages, sizes, etc.
	  o land uses
	  o proximity to employment and amenities, including travel distance and time to local employment sources and community amenities
	  o employment stability, in terms of variety of employment opportunities and industries
	  o overall appeal of the neighborhood as compared to competitive neighborhoods in the same market
	  o convenience to shopping with respect to distance, time and required means of transportation
	  o convenience to schools in terms of the distance and time for travel to school

Market Conditions (including support for the above conclusions)	• Provide relevant information in support of the conclusions relating to trends in the As-Is Property Values, demand/supply and marketing time. • Provide a description of the prevalence and impact of sales and financing concessions and/or downpayment assistance in the subject's market area. • Other areas of discussion may include Days on Market, list to sale price ratios, and/or financing availability.

Boundaries, Description and Marketing Conditions" sections of the report form.
It is clear from the three primary secondary market regulators that narrative commentary will be necessary to convey the appraiser's findings when they researched, observed and analyzed the neighborhood. One of the more definite considerations must be the boundaries. Please keep in mind, it isn't just the houses; the boundaries of a neighborhood go beyond where houses are located. Think in terms of finding a house that you would want to live in if you were locating in the urban, suburban or rural location. What would you consider were the supporting services to that location? This isn't about going to the opera, it's about proximity to necessary needs, i.e. gasoline, grocery, pharmacy, schools (depending on the demographics), hardware, proximity to connecting arteries for work, worship, hospitals, airports, recreation, etc.

When the Appraiser Practices Board (APB) was part of The Appraisal Foundation, they issued Valuation Advisories. One of the more useful publications to the residential appraiser was **Valuation Advisory number four** (Titled "[3]Identifying Comparable Properties").

"[4]....Appraisers make a distinction between the neighborhood in which a property is situated and the market area in which comparable properties will be found are located. Market area is formally defined as "the geographic or location delineation of the market for a specific category of real estate, i.e., the area in which alternative, similar properties effectively compete with the subject property in the minds of probable, potential purchasers and users. In contrast, a neighborhood is defined more generally as 'a group of complementary land uses.' In other words, the neighborhood boundaries in which the subject property is located may contain residential properties as well as non-residential properties that serve the residents of the neighborhood, whereas the boundaries of the market area for the subject property is based on the area in which similar properties compete with one another. In some cases, the subject property's neighborhood and market area may have the same boundaries, but in other cases the market area may contain several neighborhoods or portions of different neighborhoods. A market area is defined by the type of property, the type of transaction (rental or sale), the geographic area in which competition exists, and the homogeneity of properties within its boundaries."*

"...How a market area and neighborhood may be the same or differ: A subdivision comprised of tract housing of similar general design and covering ten square blocks may be a 'neighborhood' and the 'market area' if there are no other similar developments nearby. However, a 'market area' may also encompass other subdivisions that are suitable alternatives and draw from the same buyer pool as the subject, even if they are across town. The buyer pool ultimately defines the market area; if buyers consider the neighborhoods to have similar appeal, then it is likely the neighborhoods are suitable competition and could be considered within the same market area."*

..."The term market area may be more relevant to the valuation process than either neighborhood or district for several reasons:
- Using the umbrella term market area avoids the confusing and possibly negative implications of the other terms.
- A market area can include neighborhoods, districts, and combinations of both.
- Appraisers focus on market area when analyzing value influences. A market area is defined in terms of the market for a specific category of real estate and thus is the area in which alternative, similar properties effectively compete with the subject property in the minds of probable, potential purchasers and users."*

---

[3] Issue 9/26/2013

[4] There are several sources cited in this publication, "The Appraisal of Real Estate, 13rth Ed, "Market Analysis for Real Estate: Concepts and Applications in Valuation and Highest and Best Use, Appraisal Institute"; the user of this material is encouraged to go to www.appraisalfoundation.org and research this Valuation Advisory #4.

2.2   Writing Narrative Comments About The Neighborhood Analysis

When you consider the influences that create value; 1) Demand, 2) Scarcity, 3) Utility and 4) Transferability/Purchasing Power, your analysis of the neighborhood has characteristics that speak to each one of those influences.

2.2.1 Case Study – Write the characteristics that match the influences and sources of where you could obtain that information? An example is offered for each to assist your thought process.

Factor	Neighborhood Characteristic	Source
Demand	Ratio of # Listings to # Sales	MLS
Scarcity	Percentage of Built Up	Aerial Map
Utility	Proximity to Employment	City Data
Transferability	Financing Availability	Comparable Sales

2.2.2 Case Study – Using the partial sentences that convey communicating some of the key elements relevant to a residential neighborhood, finish the comment.

Demand
1.   The ratio of comparable listings to comparable sales is 8:1, _____
     _____

2.   The days on the market trend fluctuation based on the season surrounding the effective date. The effective date of this appraisal is 5/25/2017, the demand for housing
     _____

Scarcity
1.   The subdivision where the subject is located has favorable views of the natural lake with 20 lots left that actually front the water. The view of the lake extends to the houses on first and second row from the water. This feature _____
     _____

2.   There are only two High Rise Condominium Projects in the bounded neighborhood. Over the past 12 months, 2 bedroom units sell within 90 days of being listed with no concessions once placed on the market. The demand for the units is related to the _____ availability.

2.3   Factors of a Trend Analysis

Look at the One-Unit Housing Trends Block to identify key areas of where the Trend Analysis begins.

	Note: Race and the racial composition of the neighborhood are not appraisal factors.						
	Neighborhood Characteristics	**One-Unit Housing Trends**			**One-Unit Housing**	**Present Land Use %**	
N	Location ☐ Urban ☐ Suburban ☐ Rural	Property Values ☐ Increasing ☐ Stable ☐ Declining			PRICE AGE	One-Unit %	
E	Built-Up ☐ Over 75% ☐ 25-75% ☐ Under 25%	Demand/Supply ☐ Shortage ☐ In Balance ☐ Over Supply			$ (000) (yrs)	2-4 Unit %	
I G	Growth ☐ Rapid ☐ Stable ☐ Slow	Marketing Time ☐ Under 3 mths ☐ 3–6 mths ☐ Over 6 mths			Low	Multi-Family %	
H B	Neighborhood Boundaries				High	Commercial %	
O R					Pred.	Other %	
H O O D	Neighborhood Description						
	Market Conditions (including support for the above conclusions)						

Neighborhood Characteristics		
Location ☒ Urban	☐ Suburban	☐ Rural
Built-Up ☒ Over 75%	☐ 25-75%	☐ Under 25%
Growth ☐ Rapid	☒ Stable	☐ Slow

There is a relationship between the blocks and the narrative fields. Consider a report that conveys the location of the subject. Beginning with the location, identifying the neighborhood where the subject is located is over 75% built up, the focus on the more narrow district of the subject begins. Within the boundaries defined, this location has been defined by the appraiser as Urban and in the majority, built up. When analyzing the One Unit Housing Trends review the directive of the secondary market(s).

[5]*Fannie Mae Selling Guide (B4-1.3.03, Neighborhood Section of the Appraisal Report)*

Trend of Neighborhood Property Values, Demand/Supply, and Marketing Time
The appraiser must report the primary indicators of market condition for properties in the subject neighborhood as of the effective date of the appraisal by noting the information in the table below.

Trend of Property Values	**Supply of Properties in the Subject Neighborhood**	**Marketing Time for Properties**
• Increasing, • Stable, or • Declining.	• Shortage, • In-balance, or • Over-Supply.	• Under three months, • Three to six months, or • Over six months

*The appraiser's analysis of a property must take into consideration **all factors that affect value**.*

---

[5] This is an excerpt; for the full guidance go to www.efanniemae.com to secure the most recent guidance from the current Selling Guide

Because Fannie Mae purchases mortgages in all markets, this is particularly important for neighborhoods that are experiencing significant fluctuations in property values including submarkets for particular types of housing within the neighborhood. Therefore, lenders must confirm that the appraiser analyzes listings and contract sales as well as closed or settled sales, and uses the most recent and similar sales available as part of the sales comparison approach, with particular attention to sales or financing concessions in neighborhoods that are experiencing either declining property values, an over-supply of properties, or marketing times over six months. The appraiser must provide his or her conclusions for the reasons a neighborhood is experiencing declining property values, an over-supply of properties, or marketing times over six months.

When completing the One-Unit Housing Trends portion of the Neighborhood section of the appraisal report forms, the trends must be reflective of those properties deemed to be competitive to the property being appraised. If the neighborhood contains properties that are truly competitive (that is, market participants make no distinction between the properties), then all the properties within the neighborhood would be reflected in the One-Unit Housing Trends section. However, when a segmented or bifurcated market is present, the One-Unit Housing Trends portion must reflect those properties from the same segment of the market as the property being appraised. This ensures that the analysis being performed is based on competitive properties. For example, if the neighborhood contains a mix of property types not considered competitive by market participants, then a segmented or bifurcated market is *present. Additionally, the conclusions reported in this portion of the appraisal will be supported by the analysis contained in the Market Conditions Addendum to the Appraisal Report (Form 1004MC). The appraiser should also provide commentary on the other segment(s) of the neighborhood when segmentation is present.*

> *"when a segmented or bifurcated market is present, the One-Unit Housing Trends portion must reflect those properties from the same segment of the market as the property being appraised. This ensures that the analysis being performed is based on competitive properties."*

NOTICE the last sentence! "The appraiser should also provide commentary on the other segment(s) of the neighborhood when segmentation is present." It connects to the first sentence of the last paragraph under the topic, "When completing the One-Unit Housing Trends portion of the Neighborhood section of the appraisal report forms, the trends must be reflective of those properties deemed to be competitive to the property being appraised."

It is clear that from the outer boundaries of the neighborhood, the One-Unit Housing Trends is to have a "micro" focus on the residential district within the boundary that houses similar properties liken to the subject.

Consider the map below with the subject property located on a street known as W Mistletoe Avenue, in the town of San Antonio, state of TX. The subject lies west of a major interstate and east of a major discount retail center. The houses located north of the small lake range between $400K-$700K. South of the lake is a market where the prices are higher, west of Wilson Road the prices range between $30K and $200K.

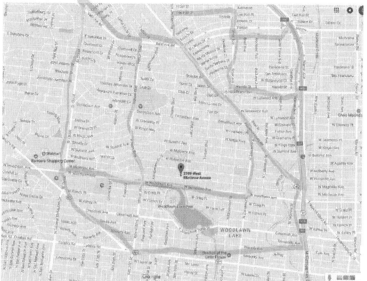

The predominant price reported in a neighborhood represents a cluster that has the greatest number of activity and majority of houses sale price within 10% from that point. The predominant price is reported at $200K. These factors illustrate a segmented market that will have differing activity. Note the report from CityData.com in the subject's zip code.

2.3.1 Case Study Exercise
Looking at the chart to the right identify the largest number of households.

_____

2.3.2 Case Study Exercise
Using a multiplier of 3 indicate the predominant price these households could afford in this zip code.

$_____ - $_____ = Predominant Range

2.3.3 Case Study Exercise
Write a brief narrative that explains the segments of the markets and what the subject's conclusion of $650,000 represents including a response to the distance the subject's concluded market value is from the predominant price calculated in the preceding Case Study Exercise (2.3.2).

Zip Code 78201 Household Income	
Income (Yr. 2015)	#Households
Less than $10,000	729
$10,000 to $14,999	1,482
$15,000 to $19,999	1,124
$20,000 to $24,999	1,143
$25,000 to $29,999	1,148
$30,000 to $34,999	843
$35,000 to $39,999	937
$40,000 to $45,999	636
$50,000 to $59,999	1,241
$60,000 to $74,999	1,128
$75,000 to $99,000	1,556
$100,000 to $124,999	596
$125,000 to $149,999	299
$150,000 to $199,999	251
$200,000 or more	120

_____
_____
_____

2.4   Linking the Neighborhood Analysis to the Highest and Best Use

HIGHEST AND BEST USE –

The USPAP demands under SR 2-2(a)(x), the appraiser summarize their support and rationale for their conclusion of Highest and Best Use. When writing comments you need to be specific.

The analysis considers first the land as vacant and then as improved even though the residential form communicates in the site section the conclusion as improved. A bit confusing, but with a carefully written summary in the addendum, the confusion can be easily remedied.

Exhibit: Consider this written addendum below that appeared in the body of an Appraisal Report

Highest & Best Use of Property if Vacant:
1. Physical Possibilities - The site has few physical restrictions other than upon the size of any possible development. This provides less than optimal access for most non-residential users, but it is typical for most residential users, as will be more fully discussed below.

2. Legal Possibilities - The site is subject to A1 zoning restrictions, as previously reported. This classification permits residential usage. According to information available to the appraiser, the property is subject to no private restrictions, and it is assumed there are none.

3. Financial Feasibility - Construction of a single-family residence would be consistent with many of the properties in the surrounding area. Residential development has continued to take place throughout the community. The residential market has been reasonably stable in the area, with no significant adverse factors influencing the overall market. The feasibility of a single-family residential development is supported by continued demand in other similar locations throughout the community. It is consistent with many surrounding properties and residential development is therefore considered feasible for the site.

4. Maximum Productivity - The site layout and location is not ideally suited for any use other than residential. No portion of the subject site is suited for agricultural income or commercial purposes. In the absence of other feasible uses, residential development is therefore considered to be most productive use for the subject site, if vacant. The zoning for the subject would seem to indicate a possible agricultural use. However, the topography of the site does not make an agricultural use feasible and the subject has no agricultural income potential.

Sounds good doesn't it? The site section below is subject for which the preceding narrative commentary was written.

Dimensions see attached parcel map			Area 55 ac		Shape irregular		View N;Woods;	
Specific Zoning Classification A1			Zoning Description Minimum Lot Size 2 acres.					
Zoning Compliance ☒ Legal ☐ Legal Nonconforming (Grandfathered Use) ☐ No Zoning ☐ Illegal (describe)								
Is the highest and best use of subject property as improved (or as proposed per plans and specifications) the present use?					☒ Yes ☐ No If No, describe See			
supplemental addendum section 4 for detailed explanation of Highest & Best Use.								
Utilities	Public	Other (describe)		Public	Other (describe)	Off-site Improvements - Type	Public	Private
Electricity	☒	☐	Water	☐	☒ well (typical)	Street Asphalt	☒	☐
Gas	☐	None	Sanitary Sewer	☐	☒ septic (typical)	Alley None	☐	☐
FEMA Special Flood Hazard Area ☐ Yes ☒ No FEMA Flood Zone X				FEMA Map # 47159C0165D			FEMA Map Date 09/29/2010	
Are the utilities and off-site improvements typical for the market area? ☒ Yes ☐ No If No, describe								
Are there any adverse site conditions or external factors (easements, encroachments, environmental conditions, land uses, etc.)?						☐ Yes ☒ No If Yes, describe		
Septic systems and private wells are typical in this area due to public water and sewer hookup being unavailable. This does not adversely affect marketability. Appraisal assumes that the well and septic are fully functional, no observable evidence of malfunction. Lack of zoning is typical in this area and does not have a negative affect on marketability. There are no restrictions that would prohibit the home from being rebuilt if destroyed.								

Remember, "as vacant" the appraiser reported: Physical Possibilities - The site has few physical restrictions other than upon the size of any possible development. This provides less than optimal access for most non-residential users, but it is typical for most residential users, as will be more fully discussed below.

Legal Possibilities - The site is subject to A1 zoning restrictions, as previously reported. This classification permits residential usage. According to information available to the appraiser, the property is subject to no private restrictions, and it is assumed there are none.

2.4.1 Case Study Exercise: Is there a connect or a disconnect between the comments in the site section and the addendum on the form?
Explain:_____
_____

Case Study Continued:

Below is the second part of the reported narrative commentary; review the information to prepare for the next exercise:

Exhibit:

Highest & Best Use of Property As Improved:

(1) Physical Possibilities - The subject was designed for single-family residential use, and it has little adaptability for other uses.

(2) Legal Possibilities - The site is subject to A1 zoning restrictions, as previously reported. This classification permits residential usage. According to information available to the appraiser, the property is subject to no private restrictions, and it is assumed there are none.

(3) Financial Feasibility - The subject's current improvements are reasonably consistent with the indicated highest and best use of the site. There are no known changes in the market that would cause this use to no longer be feasible. Vacancies have remained moderate, and some new development has continued within this sector. Recognizing the history of the subject, in conjunction with current trends in the market, a continued single-family residential use is considered to represent a feasible use for the subject property, as improved.

(4) Maximum Productivity - The existing residential improvements significantly contribute to the subject value and marketability. In addition, the site layout and location is not ideally suited for any use other than residential and no portion of the subject site is being utilized for agricultural income or commercial purposes. In the absence of other feasible uses, a continued single-family residential use is most productive for the subject.

The following page has exhibits that connect to the narrative commentary above.

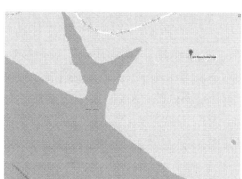

Subject Front

208 Reece Hollow Rd

Sales Price	310,000
Gross Living Area	1,014
Total Rooms	6
Total Bedrooms	3
Total Bathrooms	1.0
Location	N;Rural;
View	N;Woods;
Site	55 ac
Quality	Q4
Age	23

2.4.2 Case Study Exercise

Based on the information presented, does the highest and best use commentary convey understanding and support for the rationale of the highest and best use conclusion? __Yes or No__

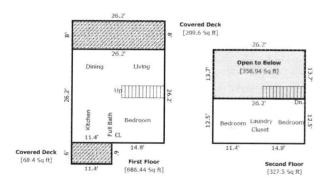

General Description		Foundation		Exterior Description	materials/condition	Interior	materials/condition
Units ☒ One ☐ One with Accessory Unit		☐ Concrete Slab ☒ Crawl Space		Foundation Walls	CB/avg	Floors	Wood-cpt
# of Stories 1.5		☐ Full Basement ☐ Partial Basement		Exterior Walls	Stn-vin/avg	Walls	drywall/avg
Type ☒ Det. ☐ Att. ☐ S-Det./End Unit		Basement Area 0 sq.ft.		Roof Surface	shingle/avg	Trim/Finish	wood/avg
☒ Existing ☐ Proposed ☐ Under Const.		Basement Finish 0 %		Gutters & Downspouts	alumn/avg	Bath Floor	Carpet/avg
Design (Style) cottage		☐ Outside Entry/Exit ☐ Sump Pump		Window Type	sngl-hung/avg	Bath Wainscot	drywall/avg
Year Built 1994		Evidence of ☐ Infestation		Storm Sash/Insulated	thermal/avg	Car Storage	☐ None
Effective Age (Yrs) 20		☐ Dampness ☐ Settlement		Screens	screens/avg	☒ Driveway # of Cars 6	
Attic ☒ None		Heating ☒ FWA ☐ HWBB ☐ Radiant		Amenities	Woodstove(s) # 0	Driveway Surface	gravel
☐ Drop Stair ☐ Stairs		☐ Other Fuel elec		☒ Fireplace(s) # 1 ☐ Fence none		☐ Garage # of Cars 0	
☐ Floor ☐ Scuttle		Cooling ☒ Central Air Conditioning		☒ Patio/Deck cv wd ☒ Porch cov wood		☐ Carport # of Cars 0	
☐ Finished ☐ Heated		☐ Individual ☐ Other		☐ Pool none ☐ Other none		☐ Att. ☐ Det. ☐ Built-in	
Appliances ☒ Refrigerator ☒ Range/Oven ☒ Dishwasher ☐ Disposal ☐ Microwave ☐ Washer/Dryer ☐ Other (describe)							
Finished area above grade contains: 6 Rooms 3 Bedrooms 1.0 Bath(s) 1,014 Square Feet of Gross Living Area Above Grade							

Note: Race and the racial composition of the neighborhood are not appraisal factors.

Neighborhood Characteristics			One-Unit Housing Trends			One-Unit Housing		Present Land Use %	
Location	☐ Urban ☐ Suburban ☒ Rural		Property Values	☐ Increasing ☒ Stable ☐ Declining		PRICE	AGE	One-Unit	10 %
Built-Up	☐ Over 75% ☐ 25-75% ☒ Under 25%		Demand/Supply	☐ Shortage ☒ In Balance ☐ Over Supply		$ (000)	(yrs)	2-4 Unit	0 %
Growth	☐ Rapid ☒ Stable ☐ Slow		Marketing Time	☐ Under 3 mths ☒ 3-6 mths ☐ Over 6 mths		19 Low 0		Multi-Family	0 %
Neighborhood Boundaries North - Kempville Hwy ; East - Smith/Trousdale County Line ; South - Cordell Hull Lake ; West - Buffalo						388 High 117		Commercial	0 %
Rd . The statistics in this section are taken from an MLS search of property within 6 mile(s) of the subject.						130 Pred. 10		Other	90 %
Neighborhood Description The subject property is located in an established residential neighborhood in the Carthag area. Schools, shops, employment centers, and related facilities are located within a 30-45 minute drive. Considering the wide ranges reported it is impossible to determine a predominant value for sales price and age. The predominant values are estimated utilizing the average and median sales prices and DOM.									
Market Conditions (including support for the above conclusions) Property values have remained stable for the past 36 months with only minor variations attributable to normal market fluctuation in an imperfect market. Supply & demand are in balance with an approximate 11 month supply of housing. MLS statistics indicate typical marketing time of less than 120 days. See Section 3 in the attached addendum for additional information.									

What additional understanding do you think should be addressed in this subject highest and best use?

_____

Chapter 3

The Narrative Support for Results of the Sales Approach

Chapter Objectives

- Consider findings of deficiencies from State Appraisal Enforcement Agencies
- Identify site fields that need expanding
- Recognize the UAD requirements in both site and improvements
- Link comments to the UAD fields

3.1 The Comparable Overview

In the valuation process after the preliminary study of sales has been performed and the final sales are selected, the appraiser will log in their final selection and begin the comparison analysis. The USPAP SR 2-2(a), states in item (v), in the comment section that enhances understanding about communicating market value, [1]"Comment: Stating the definition of value also requires any comments needed to clearly indicate to the intended users how the definition is being applied." Communication in the Appraisal Report of a market value means each step of the appraisal process performed should direct the intended users as to how the market value definition was applied. In the Sales Approach, that communication should have its focus on conveying how the adjustments were derived and conclusions resolved.

> ***Sample Comment for Addendum on Appraisal Report:***
> "Sales Approach – The appraiser began the data gathering process by researching the __(name the MLS)__ MLS system using the Polygram tool that defined the boundaries of the neighborhood selected by the appraiser. Although the parameter was a physically defined area, its determination was inclusive of search criteria for near-like characteristics bracketing GLA, Number of Bedrooms, Bathrooms, Age, Site Size and Site Amenities. Using that physical criteria, incorporating the functional, legal and economic characteristics, a cumulative gathering of data provided sales whose prices represented agreements between sellers and buyers in a competitive market of similar properties liken to the subject. Those transactions of optimum similarity were identified for the final selection to be used in the comparison approach. Market value, as defined in this report, requires the identification of central tendencies of like property types in a similar location. The differences between comparable transactions are then adjusted upward for inferior characteristics or downward for superior characteristics to create an equalization perspective between the subject and the comparable."
>
> Part of the Published Document by the Texas Appraiser Licensing and Certification Board (TALCB) asks three primary questions when investigating a complaint against an appraiser.
> 1. Is the Sales Comparison Approach Necessary for Credible Assignment Results; if not, has the appraiser explained and supported its exclusion?
> 2. Has the appraiser adequately collected, verified, and analyzed comparable sales data?
> 3. Has the appraiser employed recognized methods and techniques?

As a result of investigating allegations filed with the Board, the Oregon Appraiser Certification and Licensure Board (ACLB) Staff and Enforcement Oversight Committee developed, for informational purposes, Commonly Encountered USPAP Violations. In the Sales Approach, the following were cited:

---

[1] 2016-2017 Edition of USPAP 2-2(a)(v) comment section line numbers 699-701

Sales Comparison Section of Comparable Properties- Failing to select and/or support the selection of comparable sales using recognized methods and techniques. Some examples include:

- Leaving the subject's neighborhood when comparable sales data is readily available in the immediate neighborhood;
- Searching by price;
- Utilizing sales of superior quality, superior site characteristics, and/or superior amenities when more similar sales to the subject were readily available; and
- Lack of documentation in the workfile for the comparable sales and search criteria selected.

Sales Comparison Adjustments- Failure to support adjustments in the sales comparison approach in a market value appraisal based on recognized methods and techniques. Some examples include:

- Developing paired sales analysis but not documenting in the appraisal report and/or workfile;
- Utilizing "rules of thumb" adjustments without documenting market-based support; and
- Inadequately summarizing the information analyzed and the reasoning that supports the analysis, opinions and conclusion when using varied adjustments.

> **Question:** In your personal practice, ..., could your report and supporting workfile stand up to the test of that inquiry?

Their publication ended with, "***Most Common Encountered Error in Oregon Administrative Rule: (OAR 161-025-0060)-*** *Failing to disclose in all appraisal reports whether the comparable sales analyzed in the appraisal report were or were not confirmed by a party to the transaction or an agent or representative of a party to the transaction.*"

Question: In your personal practice, having read the most common errors by two State Appraisal Enforcement Agencies, could your report and supporting workfile stand up to the test of that inquiry?

On September 1, 2011, the Uniform Appraisal Dataset (UAD) was the mandated communication for mortgage transactions. That UAD language provided for a standardization of reading but required the appraiser to make the determination of such things as quality and condition of the improvements. The adjustment fields will contain blank fields when the comparable and the subject are the same, zeros when there are different features or aspects between the comparable and the sale that are not recognized by the buyers, and whole dollars when the different feature was recognized by the market. In the site area if the comparable is less than one acre the square feet are expressed without commas for ease of the software readers.

3.2 Line items of the Sales Comparison Approach

There is a process, a line-up, as you will, for the items of comparison. Your comments should reflect the communication of the item requiring adjustment as well as how the adjustment was derived albeit, quantified through paired sales or regression or a qualified judgment. One of the more common mistakes appraisers will make is they will develop a "boilerplate" of commentary on their narrative addendum to support their thought process and sources for adjustment. Although that seems like a great idea, when it's not specific to the assignment, it shows a lack of effort on the appraiser's behalf to communicate relevant information. When there appears a page or greater listing all the adjustment lines in the Sales Grid of the appraisal forms, citing how the adjustments were derived and applied and yet only three adjustments were necessary, clearly this is "canned language" that is not relevant to the assignment. It also casts doubt on if the appraiser actually did go into the market and verify a market reaction. That's when a cross-check with the workfile is made. If there is no proof of an analysis of the sales in that market for that assignment, then the charges begin to build beginning with "no support for the adjustments". Appraisal services are important to the day to day mortgage lending world. However, paying someone for their unsupported opinion makes the computer-generated report very attractive.

Investigators of Mortgage Fraud has identified triggers that signal when a fraud is being implemented. Their findings are the adjustments above the room count and GLA area. For that reason, the appraiser needs to be very careful about the details of their communication for those areas above that line item that may need to be adjusted.

Exhibit 3.1   Line Items of the URAR Form Sale Price - Data Sources - Concessions

FEATURE	SUBJECT			COMPARABLE SALE # 1		
Address						
Proximity to Subject						
Sale Price	$					$
Sale Price/Gross Liv. Area	$		sq. ft.	$		sq. ft.
Data Source(s)						
Verification Source(s)						
VALUE ADJUSTMENTS	DESCRIPTION			DESCRIPTION		+(-) $ Adjustment
Sale or Financing Concessions						
Date of Sale/Time						
Location						
Leasehold/Fee Simple						
Site						
View						
Design (Style)						
Quality of Construction						
Actual Age						
Condition						
Above Grade Room Count	Total	Bdrms.	Baths	Total	Bdrms.	Baths
Gross Living Area		sq. ft.			sq. ft.	
Basement & Finished Rooms Below Grade						
Functional Utility						
Heating/Cooling						
Energy Efficient Items						
Garage/Carport						
Porch/Patio/Deck						
Net Adjustment (Total)				☐ + ☐ -		$
Adjusted Sale Price of Comparables				Net Adj.	%	
				Gross Adj.	%	$

Sale Price of the Subject must match the sale price in the contract section if a sale is pending. If a comparable sold in a reported dollars and cents, round up. If it is a listing or a pending contract price, report the list price or offered price.

Data Sources – Too many appraisers rely on their software to catch UAD errors. The current UAD manual should be the basis for the entry. There is a specific format that is being asked under the UAD specification.

The entry needs to include first the identified MLS system and then the Days on the Market. For example, if it were Houston and the MLS number was 56892 and the days on the market were 110 it would be reported as HAR#5682;DOM110

3.2.1 Exercise: Circle which of the examples below shows compliance with UAD requirements?

Data Source(s)		Austin MLS #7010219;DOM 143	Austin MLS #4793298;DOM 83	Austin MLS #2180506;DOM 59
Verification Source(s)		CAD-Keller Williams Realty	CAD-RE/Max	CAD-Keller Williams Realty

Data Source(s)		MLS 102367;DOM 221	MLS 102239;DOM 146	MLS 102314;DOM 125
Verification Source(s)		UCAD	UCAD	UCAD

Data Source(s)		SABOR MLS #886179;DOM 184	SABOR MLS #911252;DOM 74	Settlement Statement;DOM Unk
Verification Source(s)		Tax Record	Tax Record	Tax Record

Exhibit 3.2   Line Items of the URAR Form Sale Concessions

FEATURE	SUBJECT	COMPARABLE SALE # 1	
Address			
Proximity to Subject			
Sale Price	$	$	
Sale Price/Gross Liv. Area	$ sq. ft.	$ sq. ft.	
Data Source(s)			
Verification Source(s)			
VALUE ADJUSTMENTS	DESCRIPTION	DESCRIPTION	+(-) $ Adjustment
Sale or Financing Concessions			
Date of Sale/Time			
Location			
Leasehold/Fee Simple			
Site			
View			
Design (Style)			
Quality of Construction			
Actual Age			
Condition			
Above Grade	Total	Bdrms.	Baths Total	Bdrms.	Baths	
Room Count			
Gross Living Area	sq. ft.	sq. ft.	
Basement & Finished Rooms Below Grade			
Functional Utility			
Heating/Cooling			
Energy Efficient Items			
Garage/Carport			
Porch/Patio/Deck			
Net Adjustment (Total)		☐ + ☐ -	$
Adjusted Sale Price of Comparables		Net Adj. % Gross Adj. %	$

NOTE: Many appraisers fail to read and communicate the directive when "below-market" financing exists. Below market financing can have an impact on the market values which equates to a significant factor of communication. *A little-known fact that is right under the nose of appraisers is the statement made in the UAD manual*. "The appraiser must indicate if sales transactions with below-market financing are used for comparable sales."

Sale Concessions – The UAD has directives for the larger adjustment field box. Its directives are very clear:

Line 1 – Indicate sale type for each comp.
Valid entries are:

- REO Sale
- Short Sale
- Court Ordered Sale
- Estate Sale
- Relocation Sale
- Non-Arms Length Sale
- Listing

*Note-you can report any other relevant information including whether more than one sale type applies, elsewhere in the appraisal report.

Line 2 – You must enter the financing type from the approved list AND the total amount of the concessions for each settled sale. If there are no concessions, then enter zero (0).

Financing Type
- FHA
- VA
- Conventional
- Seller
- Cash
- USDA-Rural housing
- Other-appraiser to enter description if not on this list, ensuring the text fits in allowable space.

Reporting Format Example
Line 1: ArmLth
Line 2: FHA;5000

3.2.2   Writing Comments for Sales Concessions

The key to writing comments for sales concessions is to communicate how and why the concessions were made. There have been so many communications and passionate expressions about the subject, the appraiser needs to consider the highlighted points of input. As one appraiser touted "a concession is part of the deal, not part of the value."

[2]**Fannie Mae's Highlights**: "The appraiser must consider the impact a sales concession had on the transaction. The adjustments must reflect the difference between what the comparables actually sold for with the sales concessions, and what they would have sold for without the concessions, so the dollar amount of the adjustments will approximate the reaction of the market to the concessions."

[3]**FHA Highlights**: "Sales concessions influence the price paid for real estate. It may be in the form of loan discount points, loan origination fees, settlement assistance, payment of condo/PUD fees, builder incentives or the inclusion of non-realty items in the transaction.

Appraisers are required to verify and analyze all sales on a cash-equivalent basis (interest rate buy-downs, below market financing, owner financing, etc.). As stated in the Appraisal of Real estate, Eleventh Edition:

"In cash equivalency analysis, an appraiser investigates the sales price of comparable properties that appear to have been sold with non-market financing, to determine whether adjustments to reflect typical market terms are warranted. First, sales with non-market financing are compared to other sales transacted with market financing to determine whether an adjustment for cash equivalency can be made. Market evidence is always the best indicator of such an adjustment. However, buyers rarely, if ever, rely on strict dollar for dollar cash equivalency adjustments."

The appraiser must verify all sales transactions for seller concessions and report those findings on the URAR. The amount of the negative adjustment to be made to each comparable with sales or financing concessions is equal to any increase in the purchase price of the comparable that the appraiser determines to be attributable to the concessions. [4]It should be noted that the need to make negative adjustments and the amount of the adjustments to the comparables for sales and financing concessions are not based on how typical the concession might be for a segment of the market (large sales concessions can be relatively typical in a particular segment of the market and still result in sales prices that reflect more than the value of the real estate). The adjustment must reflect the difference between what the concessions actually sold for with the sales concessions and what they would have sold for without the concessions so that the

---

[2] March 2009 FAQs Appraisal and Property Report Policies and Forms
[3] FHA Single Family Appraisal System, March 24, 2000 SASS FAQs #31
[4] Although this is an FHA highlight subsequent publications of Fannie Mae reiterated almost verbatim this communication

dollar amount of the adjustments will approximate the reaction of the market to the concessions.

Writing the comment
Example: "The appraiser has reported the adjustments paid by the seller towards financing. The adjustment is in the amount that reflects what the appraiser believes has impacted the price. No adjustment is made for the sales concessions of minor personal property (identify if appliances or other concessions were part of the sale) which also were part of the exchange as of the date of the contract and passed on the settled closed date."

Make a mental note, don't make an adjustment that you cannot prove in your workfile was reasoned by your comparison and reconciliation. It should never be an arbitrary percentage such as many canned comments will often state, "Concessions are considered normal up to 3%, anything over is adjusted downward for its inflation." It's a poor execution of diligence when the appraiser makes this type of comment and none of the sales had concessions. The workfiles are examined for notes and highlights of concessions paid and the analysis of the dominance of concessions. Lack of a printout indicating the research into sales where concessions were reported fails the evidence of the "reasonableness" in performing the contract analysis as well as the impact of concessions on a sale price.

> "... mental note, don't make an adjustment that you cannot prove in your workfile was reasoned by your comparison and reconciliation.

3.3   Line items of the Sales Comparison Approach – Date of Sale/Time

During the 1980s, adjustment for period differences between the effective date and the settled closed dates were common as the market was quickly shifting downward. A great deal of emphasis on identifying downward values with Market Conditions due to the housing crisis of 2007-2008 was experienced. It was that economic crisis that prompted the 1004 Mortgage Conditions (MC) form. When writing the Appraisal Report, there needs to be consistency found in:

- 1004MC – Is the trend indicating a stable market or one that is changing upward or downward

and

- Neighborhood One-Unit Housing Trends – Indication of values correlates also to the marketing time reported for comparable listings

If the report shows the market is changing and the comparable sale falls outside the effective date month, an adjustment will be expected in the field. If the market trends are communicated to be stable in the value, and are close in the time frame of comparison (within the past year) there will not be an adjustment but the field needs to reflect that observation. The appraiser confirms that lack of market reaction by putting a zero in the adjustment field.

> ***Keep in mind:***
> - Comparable Sale closed outside the effective date month but no adjustment required
>   - ***ZERO goes in field***
>
> - Comparable Sale closed inside the same effective date month no adjustment is required
>   - ***Field is left BLANK***
>
> - Comparable Sale closed outside the effective date month in a changing market
>   - ***Adjustment required***

3.4   Line items of the Sales Comparison Approach – Location/Site/View

Which comes first, is it the chicken or the egg, the location, site size or the view? It's important first to understand the difference between the location reported in the neighborhood section of residential form reports and the location in the Sales Approach on residential appraisal report forms. They're not always the same.

In the neighborhood section that identifies the location, it is speaking of the bounded areas defined. Therefore, when the Sales Approach is being performed and the location is being identified, the sales would come from a similar location. However, there can be location differences within the same neighborhood. In many neighborhoods, there will be lots that have "situs" characteristics, i.e. prime location. The rules for determining situs vary between jurisdictions and can depend on the context, but, under English law, in general:
- the situs of real estate(land) is where the land is located

The appraiser will often state that there is no credible way to separate why someone would pay a different price when waterfront properties are purchased and compared with non-waterfront lots as the location, site and view are all part of the price paid. When certain site characteristics house prime factors of demand such as waterfront, then the view will trend to be part of the demand and can sometimes play second to the site area such as the waterfront feet.

Another challenge of the UAD is the reporting of the site area. If the site is less than one acre its reported in square feet; if it's greater than one acre, it's reported in acreage limited to two decimals. When there is a mixture of both square feet and acreage it can be difficult not to put in zeros in those sites reporting in square feet. For adherence to UAD there must be that reporting without the commas.

3.4.1 *Exercise:* What's wrong with the UAD communication of the grid?

Answer: _____

VALUE ADJUSTMENTS	DESCRIPTION	DESCRIPTION	+(-) $ Adjustment	DESCRIPTION	+(-) $ Adjustment	DESCRIPTION	+(-) $ Adjustment
Sales or Financing		ArmLth		ArmLth		ArmLth	
Concessions		VA;0	0	Conv;0	0	VA;0	0
Date of Sale/Time		s10/11;c08/11	0	s03/12;c02/12	0	s04/12;c02/12	0
Location	N;Res;	N;Res;		N;Res;		N;Res;	
Leasehold/Fee Simple	Fee Simple	Fee Simple		Fee Simple		Fee Simple	
Site	1.23 ac	21,344 sf	7500	24,394 sf	7500	21,344 sf	7500
View	N;Res;	N;Res;		N;Res;		N;Res;	
Design (Style)	Ranch	Ranch		Contemporary	0	Mediterranean	0
Quality of Construction	Q2	Q2		Q3	12000	Q3	12000
Actual Age	0	0		6	6000	7	7000
Condition	C1	C1		C2	0	C2	0
Above Grade	Total / Bdrms. / Baths	Total / Bdrms. / Baths		Total / Bdrms. / Baths		Total / Bdrms. / Baths	
Room Count	11 / 4 / 3.1	11 / 5 / 4.1	-5000	10 / 4 / 4.0	-3500	9 / 4 / 3.1	0
Gross Living Area	4339 sq.ft.	4499 sq.ft.	-10400	4277 sq.ft.	4030	3971 sq.ft.	23920

Writing the Comment

Example #1 (multiple factors are integrated)
The subject has integrating relevant site characteristics that impact the demand; 1) Waterfront Feet, 2) View, 3) Location. The subject fronts a large man-made lake that identifies this location known as Magnolia Waters placing it in high demand. The lake was built to have many inlets which magnify the number of potential waterfront lots available due to its irregular shape. There is an island in the center of the lake which is not available for purchase or development, considered common area for which the annual Homeowners Association is responsible and gives each lot a waterfront view and a natural habitat. *The adjustment for these sites are made to the waterfront feet as there are varied prices, but the view and the location are in essence the same for all comparable waterfront lots.*

Example #2 (multiple factors are integrated)
The subject has integrating relevant site characteristics that impact the demand; 1) Waterfront Feet, 2) View, 3) Location. The subject fronts a large man-made lake that identifies this location known as Magnolia Waters placing it in high demand. The lake was built to have many inlets which magnify the number of potential waterfront lots available due to its irregular shape. There is an island in the center of the lake which is not available for purchase or development, considered common area for which the annual Homeowners Association is responsible and gives each lot a waterfront view and a natural habitat. *The differences between those sites on the water versus the one comparable sale that is not on the water was made in the location field and based on the differences of the lot value.*

Example #3 (location factors)
The subject and Sale #1 are both located in the same neighborhood. Lack of available sales in the neighborhood directed the appraiser to research comparable competing markets. Sale #2 was distanced 10 miles north but similar in its size with similar designed detached single-family residences. The higher tax rate and higher cost proved

the location to be slightly superior concluded at $4,000 higher as a result of the location. Sale #3 was 5 miles west in a competing market slightly inferior having different school district and lots that range $2,500 to $3,200 less than sites in the subject's immediate neighborhood concluded at $3,000 less for the inferior location adjustment. The varied differences in site sizes are not the impacting factor for price differences, hence adjustment for site sizes are not made.

3.5   Line items of the Sales Comparison Approach – Quality of Construction

In April 2012, there was a new UAD Manual published which clarified both Quality of Construction and Condition. Both of these items now have requirements of being reported as a rating versus text communication.

Excerpt of the April 2012 UAD Standardization Requirement
(circled areas are the revised directives as of 04/19/2012)

Quality of Construction

The appraiser must select one quality rating from the list below for the subject property and each comparable property. The appraiser must indicate the quality rating that best describes the overall quality of the property. Only one selection is permitted. The quality rating for the subject property must describe the overall quality of the property as-of the effective date of the appraisal and the overall quality of each comparable property as-of the date of sale for the comparable properties on an absolute basis, not on a relative basis or how the properties relate to other properties in the neighborhood.

- Q1
- Q2
- Q3
- Q4
- Q5
- Q6

The definitions for the quality ratings are provided in Exhibit 1.

Reporting Format:
Quality of Construction – Appraiser must select one value from the specified list

In certain locations, there can be differences in quality of construction within the same neighborhood. Remember that quality of construction bases its conclusion on parameters set forth by the developers of the UAD.

Quality Ratings and Definitions

Q1

Dwellings with this quality rating are usually unique structures that are individually designed by an architect for a specified user. Such residences typically are constructed from detailed architectural plans and specifications and feature an exceptionally high level of workmanship and exceptionally high-grade materials throughout the interior and exterior of the structure. The design features exceptionally high-quality exterior refinements and ornamentation, and exceptionally high-quality interior refinements. The workmanship, materials, and finishes throughout the dwelling are of exceptionally high quality.

Q2

Dwellings with this quality rating are often custom designed for construction on an individual property owner's site. However, dwellings in this quality grade are also found in high-quality tract developments featuring residence constructed from individual plans or from highly modified or upgraded plans. The design features detailed, high quality exterior ornamentation, high-quality interior refinements, and detail. The workmanship, materials, and finishes throughout the dwelling are generally of high or very high quality.

Q3

Dwellings with this quality rating are residences of higher quality built from individual or readily available designer plans in above-standard residential tract developments or on an individual property owner's site. The design includes significant exterior ornamentation and interiors that are well finished. The workmanship exceeds acceptable standards and many materials and finishes throughout the dwelling have been upgraded from "stock" standards.

Q4

Dwellings with this quality rating meet or exceed the requirements of applicable building codes. Standard or modified standard building plans are utilized and the design includes adequate fenestration and some exterior ornamentation and interior refinements. Materials, workmanship, finish, and equipment are of stock or builder grade and may feature some upgrades.

Q5

Dwellings with this quality rating feature economy of construction and basic functionality as main considerations. Such dwellings feature a plain design using readily available or basic floor plans featuring minimal fenestration and basic finishes with minimal exterior ornamentation and limited interior detail. These dwellings meet minimum building codes and are constructed with inexpensive, stock materials with limited refinements and upgrades.

Q6

Dwellings with this quality rating are of basic quality and lower cost; some may not be suitable for year-round occupancy. Such dwellings are often built with simple plans or without plans, often utilizing the lowest quality building materials. Such dwellings are often built or expanded by persons who are professionally unskilled or possess only minimal construction skills. Electrical, plumbing, and other mechanical systems and equipment may be minimal or non-existent. Older dwellings may feature one or more substandard or non-conforming additions to the original structure

Writing Comments about Quality

Since the inception of UAD the description of Quality is more defined. It is this basis that the appraiser can develop their comments.

Example: "The UAD communication mandated ratings be given on quality of construction for the benefit of standardization. The challenge is there are no allowances for quality combinations and must be concluded on one sole rating. The appraiser has determined the rating based on the dominance of characterization. When there were obvious market recognized differences that were isolated to quality of construction, as seen in Sale #3, which did not qualify for a whole rating point upward or downward, the dollars associated with that slight difference was made. This was necessary on Sale #3 that had one room which was above a Q3 in that it was recently upgraded with superior custom finishes easily recognized in its quick sale at its market price. The quick absorption equated to a .5% of the Price less land Value downward adjustment for its superior quality. That adjustment was based on the Days-On-Market (DOM) being just under 2 months and the verification of reaction based on the listing realtor. When compared to typical DOM that percentage difference was extracted."

3.6   Line items of the Sales Comparison Approach – Condition

In April 2012, there was a clarification of the condition rating with similar directives as seen in the quality of construction. The rating needs to be specific to the property, an absolute and not a cumulative comparison of the transactions used in the Sales Approach.

It's important to ensure that when condition is being spoken of, your comments reflect the absolute of each transaction.

Note below an excerpt of an appraisal that reports varied condition ratings with interior photograph of the living room and the kitchen.

Actual Age	6
Condition	C2

Sample Comments:
"Based on the actual age the subject would normally begin to show signs of wear and tear. The subject has been well maintained and has no signs of its physical six years. Based on the observation coupled with the age the appraiser has concluded the condition rating of C2."

3.7   Line items of the Sales Comparison Approach – Age

There is no reporting of both actual and effective age under the UAD. The directive is to report the actual age and for new construction less than one year of age the number "0" is to be entered as the age. When the age is uncertain then the tilde symbol ~ is used. The question is when does age difference become necessary to adjust and how does the appraiser support the evidence of a market that reacts for the actual age differences? Factors to consider:

- Actual Age isn't Effective Age-there is no evidence of how maintenance impacted the market reaction to any differences

- Condition, although absolute in its determination, cannot be isolated as a measure across the board to encompass age. For example, a 25-year-old house well maintained in average condition will not be the same as a 10-year-old house well maintained in average condition.

- Using mechanical dollar adjustments of $1,000 per year of actual age has no basis if not supported by analytical studies

Consider the following case study in how an age reaction can be extracted:

	Sale 2	Sale 3		
Sale price	$83,300	$74,000		
Concessions	3300	2000	Subtract	
Subtotal	$80,000	$72,000		
Land Value	15,000	15,000	Subtract	
Subtotal	$65,000	$57,000		
Adjust for GLA			Difference	
GLA	1241	1166	75 GLA S.F.	
$30.81 pGLA SF difference	0	+2310.75	(30.81x75)	Pre-determined sf adj. x difference
Subtotal	$65,000	$59,311	$5,689	Difference in Sale 2 & Sale 3 after adjusting for SF @ $30.81 sf
Age Difference	29	35	6	Difference in their actual ages
Percent Difference				
Dollar Difference			$5,689	
Improvement Present Worth			$59,311	(5,689 ÷ 59,311 = 0.09591813 total)
Percent Difference			0.09591813	
Age Difference			6	
Per year reaction			**0.01598635**	Conclusion of 0.09591813 ÷ 6 years

The assumption here is that no updates to either sale have taken place. Another alternative would be to develop effective ages and compare in a similar manner. The alternative would require an entry on one of the blank lines at the bottom of the grid of the Sales Comparison and a narrative comment on how this was achieved.

Once the extracted reaction is determined, the application would require adjusting the sales to the subject for the difference, but only after the sales prices of the comparable transactions were adjusted for their present worth (sale price less land value which includes landscaping less site improvement). Once the present worth is concluded, the percent per year of difference between the comparable sale and the subject is applied. In the example, based on the preceding example, the per-year reaction is 0.016 rounded multiplied by the present worth after GLA.

Example:

	Subject	Sale #1	Sale #2	Sale #3	Sale #4	
Sale Price	$99,500.00	$89,900.00	$83,300.00	$74,000.00	$89,900.00	
less land value	$15,000.00	$13,692.00	$9,500.00	$13,000.00	$13,000.00	includes landscaping
less Fence	$2,000	$2,000	$1,800	$1,400	$2,000	
Present Worth		$74,208	$72,000.00	$59,600	$74,900	Subtotal after deduction
GLA	1434	1396	1241	1166	1313	
GLA difference	N/A	38	193	268	121	
Adj. GLA 30.81	N/A	$1,170.78	$5,946.33	$8,257.08	$3,728.01	Adjustment in this case all negative
Present Worth	N/A	$75,378.78	$77,946.33	$67,857.08	$78,628.01	Subtotal before age
Actual Age	37	36	29	35	28	
Difference in yr.'s age		1	8	2	9	
Adjust @ 1.6% per yr.	N/A	$1,206.06	$9,977.13	$2,171.43	$11,322.43	Age Adjustment

Only the adjustments would show on the Sales Comparison Approach-this sheet would go into your workfile to show how you reasoned through the adjustment. With accounting spreadsheet software such as Excel this takes minimal time.

3.8   Line items of the Sales Comparison Approach – GLA

In the example above there was an extracted age which resulted when other major items were adjusted. This chapter has presented the adjustments discussion in the order of the grid in the Sales Approach on residential forms. When performing the paired sales, the order is dictated by the identification of those sales with the least number of dissimilar characters. Notice below where two comparisons are made and both are sizably different in their reaction. When there are few comparisons to be made due to the limited number of sales and there is a broad range of notable reaction, a weighted approach can reconcile the indicators of the comparison.

Paired Sales

Sq. Ft. Adjustment

	Sale #1	Sale #2	Sale #3	Sale #4
Sale Price	$89,900.00	$83,300.00	$74,000.00	$89,900.00
Concessions	3900	3300	2000	3850
Site	.23 acres	.146 acres	.17 acres	.20 acres
Site Value	$13,700	$9,500	$11,100	$13,000
Extracted				
Improvement	$72,300	$70,500	$60,900	$60,900
Sq. Ft. GLA	1396	1241	1166	1313

	Sale #1	Sale #2		Difference
Sale Price	$89,900.00	$83,300.00		
Concessions	3900	3300		
Site	.23 acres	.146 acres		
Site Value	$13,700.00	$9,500.00		
Extracted				
Improvement	$72,300.00	$70,500.00		$1,800.00
Sq. Ft. GLA	1396	1241		155
				$11.61

	Sale #1		Sale #3	Difference
Sale Price	$89,900.00		$74,000.00	
Concessions	3900		2000	
Site	.23 acres		.17 acre	
Site Value	13700		$11,100	
Extracted				
Improvement	$72,300.00		$60,900	$11,400
Sq. Ft. GLA	1396		1166	230
				$50

This comparison shown was disqualified in the conclusion believing the major reason for the difference was due to the age dissimilarity as opposed to the Gross Living Area (GLA) difference.

	Sale #1	Sale #4
Sale Price	89900	89900
Concessions	3900	3850
Site	.23 acres	.20 acres
Site Value Extracted	13700	13000
Improvement	72300	60900
Sq. Ft. GLA	1396	1313

Size difference is too small, difference price is attributable to age

Conclusions by Weighting Comparisons
If both conclusions are given equal weight, the concluded GLA adjustment would be:

Comparisons #1	$11.61 x 50% =	$ 5.81
Comparison #2	$50.00 x 50% =	+25.00
Conclusion of Sq. Ft. Adjustment for GLA	=	$30.81

Writing the Comment-
If the analysis that concluded the square foot adjustment by a similar quantified analysis, commentary is necessary to convey how the adjustment was derived. In quantified analysis such as paired sales and regression conclusions, the market reactions to differences are identified. If the analysis included a consideration of a regression analysis was performed it must also be communicated. For example, "The appraiser utilized paired sales, multiple regression analysis as well as the percentage breakdown comparison (segmenting the sale between land contribution, site improvement contribution as well as the main improvement for a closer comparison; a form of paired sales). A reconciliation between those indicators was made and utilized to conclude the reported adjustments in the Sales Comparison Approach."

Quantified Analysis Paired Sale Comment-
"The appraiser considered within the sales found suitable for comparative analysis and found two conclusions that were weighted and reconciled at $30.81 per square foot for GLA."

Quantified Regression Analysis Overview

Before you can comment you need to have a basic understanding of the terms of a regression analysis. Regression analysis is a statistical process that establishes relationships between a set of variables. In regression analysis, there is a dependent variable (the actual problem you're trying to solve) and independent variable(s). In a linear regression for real property value, for example, the depending variable would be the value and the independent variable may be the GLA. The formula that is embedded in accounting programs such as Excel would be:

$$y = a + bx$$

- y is the dependent variable
- x is the independent variable
- a is a constant
- b is the slope of the line

For every increase of 1 in x, y will change by an amount that is equal to b. For example, if you know the base value and the number of square feet of GLA, you can predict the value of property if there are no other major differences in the relevant characteristics.

One of the measures of how well the statistical model explains the data is the R^2 value. For example, an R2 of .72 means that 72% of the variance in the observed values of the dependent variable is explained by the model, and 28% of the differences remain unexplained in the error term.

The "error term" is a variable in a statistical model that is created when the model doesn't fully represent the actual relationship between the independent variable and the dependent variable. The result of the incomplete relationship, i.e. the "error term", is the amount in which the equation may differ during the empirical analysis. The error term is also known as the "residual", or the "remainder" term.

In simple terms, it means the model will not be completely accurate, and will result in differing results during the real-world applications.

$$Y = a\chi + bp + \varepsilon$$

Symbols explained

Y = dependent variable

a, b = constants

χ, p = independent variables

ε = error term

When the actual "Y" is different from the "Y" in the model during an empirical test, then the error term will not be equal to 0. That result means there are other factors that influence the "Y".

Each independent variable will also have another number that is attached to it in the regression results. That number is called its "p-value" or significance level. The "p-value" is also a percentage that tells you how probable it is that the coefficient for that independent variable emerged by chance and does not describe a real relationship. For example, a p-value of 0.10 means there is a 10% chance that the relationship emerged randomly and a 90% chance that the relationship is real. Generally, the accepted practice is to consider variables with a "p-value" of less than .1 as significant.

Writing the comment explaining the output needs to be simply conveyed as the mathematical understanding behind regression analysis is beyond the understanding of most users of appraisal services. It is for this reason that charts often offer a better view of the output. Even with charts the appraiser needs to communicate why there is strength in the output.

Example: "The regression output of the sales approach considered _____ sales. Confidence in the output was measured at 90% meaning there was 10% of the differences that were unexplained. In residential valuation, there will always be a certain amount of unexplained variables/differences as the data that is reported will never completely communicate all of the details or reasons for the purchase. This regression analysis was not solely relied upon, rather it was a tool of support that was used to aid the appraiser in making the final determination of the market value based on all of the analyses and approach(es) to value used in this assignment."

3.9   Line items of the Sales Comparison Approach – Room Count

The room count communicates Total Number of Rooms, Bedrooms and Baths. In most residential properties of average to good quality the number of rooms isn't as important as the functional floor plan layout and the number of bedrooms and proportionate number of baths. In most cases, the overall number of rooms is not the reaction seen in the market; rather it is the GLA. However, when the specific type of room such as bedroom count is viewed, there will be a market reaction incrementally.

Consider this chart of a zip code area taken from City-Data.com which is a census count that is periodically updated.

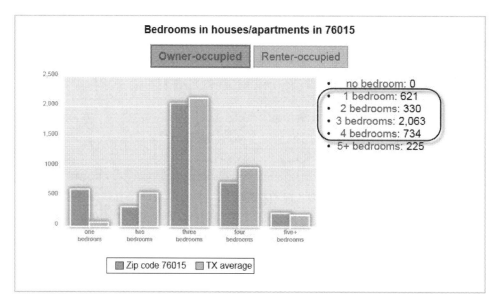

Because the chart shows both houses and apartments, the key tabs "Owner-Occupied" data is shown. This clearly shows the demand of residents is the 3-bedroom home. The secondary distinction could be an income approach. Although the area may be primarily owner-occupied, there is generally some rental information available for housing that will show differences in gross monthly rent on a "per bedroom" basis. In many instances, there may be rental information, but not sales, that shows tenant occupancy which can be interpolated with the verified sales which are not tenant occupied. The word "interpolate" means to introduce other elements.

Example:

Median Rental #1	2 Bedroom	Gross Monthly Rent	$ 850
Median Rental #2	3 Bedroom	Gross Monthly Rent	$1,050
Median Sale Price	2 Bedroom		$75,000
Median Sale Price	3 Bedroom		$86,600

GRM Interpolation

Median Sale Price 2 Bedroom$75,000 ÷ 850 Median Rent 2-Bedroom = 88.24

Median Sale Price 3 Bedroom $86,600 ÷$1,050 Median Rent 3-Bedrm = 82.48

Reaction of rental difference

$1050 Gross Monthly Rent 3 Bedroom

$ 850 Gross Monthly Rent 2 Bedroom

$ 200

Comparative Reasoning #1

Rental Difference of 2 Bedroom versus 3 Bedroom	$200
X GRM of Two Bedroom	x 88.24
Reaction	$17,648

Comparative Reasoning #2

Rental Difference of 2 Bedroom versus 3 Bedroom	$200
X GRM of Three Bedroom	x 82.48
Reaction	$16,496

Comparative Reasoning #3

Difference in Median Sale Price of 2-Bedroom versus 3 Bedroom

3 Bedroom	$86,600
2 Bedroom	$75,000
Reaction	$11,600

There are three perspectives of a reaction. The challenge with this analysis is the reality that GLA may also be a factor. The question to answer is two-fold:

1. Is there evidence the market has a preference of 3 bedrooms versus 2 bedrooms?

    YES

2. Is there reason to believe the purchase of the dwelling would consider both the GLA size and the number of bedrooms?   Not yet proven

    Consider the median sales prices of concluded of both the 2-bedroom versus 3-bedroom GLA.

2-Bedroom Median GLA	1,100
3-Bedroom Median GLA	1,250
Difference	150 Sq. Ft.

    If the extracted per sq. ft. for GLA is $31.80 per square foot, apply that to the area of difference and then deduct it from the perspective of the three comparatives analyses.

2 Bedroom Median GLA		1,100
3 Bedroom Median GLA		1,250
Difference		150 Sq. Ft
GLA difference		x $31.80
Impact of market reaction on GLA of additional Bedroom		$4,770

	Comparative #1	Comparative #2	Comparative #3
	$17,648	$16,496	$11,600
Adjustment GLA	- 4,770	- 4,770	- 4,770
Conclusion	$12,878	$11,726	$11,130

Writing the Comment

The appraiser considered the additional reaction of bedroom differences. The studies showed a strong reaction between 2-bedroom versus 3-bedroom, but no major reaction between 3-bedroom versus 4-bedroom. Sale #4 was used for the basis of bracketing the square footage of GLA. Sale #4 was a 2 Bedroom and the smallest square footage of GLA. When comparative analysis was performed the reaction beyond the GLA on a 3 bedroom versus a 2 bedroom ranged between $11,130 - $12,878 reconciled, at $12,000.

3.10 Reconciling the Value Conclusion of the Sales Comparison Approach

There are varied conclusions when the Sales Approach is performed and often the appraiser questions where the value should be when having to conclude one number. In some circumstances, a weighted analysis can be of assistance. There are many ways to weight the approach. The subsequent page will show four weighted techniques:

1. Net Dollars Weighted Analysis – A factor is derived from the relationship between the sale price unadjusted, the net dollars of adjustment and the reconciled net adjusted value.

2. Gross Dollars Weighted Analysis – A factor is derived from the relationship between the sale price unadjusted and the gross dollars used to derive the net adjusted value. The strength is in the least gross dollars used to adjust the comparable sales to a net adjusted value.

3. Number of Adjustments Weighted Analysis – A factor is derived from the number of times the comparable was adjusted. The theory in this analysis is that the least number of times the sale is adjusted the greater the weight of the indicated net adjusted price is in the final value.

4. Percentage Contribution – This is a weighting of each net adjusted sale. Given the other considerations of net dollars, gross dollars and number of adjustment the percentages are assigned and applied to the adjusted, sales price for a contribution of all sales to the final value.

Note the subsequent page for an illustration of how these weighted analyses can aid the appraiser in finalizing their value conclusion.

Weighted Analysis						
Weighted by # of Adjustments						
	Sale #1	Sale #2	Sale #3	Sale #4	Total of	
Sale Price per Thousand	89.9	83.3	74	89.9		
÷ Number of Adjustments	2	3	3	3		
Factor	44.95	27.76667	24.66667	29.96667	127.35	Weighted Total Factor
Adjusted Sale Price	$85,000	$77,725	$77,700	$76,275		
Extension of Factor x Adj. SP	$3,820,750	$2,158,164.17	$1,916,600.00	$2,285,707.50	$10,181,221.67	Weighted Total Extension
					$79,946.77	Conclusion of WTE divided by WTF
Weighted by Net $'s						
	Sale #1	Sale #2	Sale #3	Sale #4		
Sale Price	$89,900	$83,300	$74,000	$89,900		
÷ Net Dollars Adjusted	4900	5575	3700	13625		
Conclusion of Factor	18.346939	14.94	20.00	6.60	59.886808	Weighted Total Factor
Adjusted Sale Price	$85,000.00	$77,725.00	$77,700.00	$76,275.00		
Extension of Factor x Adj. SP	$1,559,489.80	$1,161,343.95	$1,554,000.00	$503,275.05	$4,778,108.79	Weighted Total Sum of Extension
					$79,785.66	Conclusion of WTSE divided by WTF

Weighted by Gross $'s						
	Sale #1	Sale #2	Sale #3	Sale #4		
Sale Price	$89,900.00	$83,300.00	$74,000.00	$89,900.00		
÷ Gross Dollars	$4,900	$15,225	$9,700	$19,675		
Factor conclusion	18.34693878	5.471264368	7.628865979	4.569250318	36.01631944	Weighted Total Factor
Adjusted Sale Price	$85,000	$77,725	$77,700	$76,275		
Extension of factor x Adj. SP	$1,559,489.80	$425,254.02	$592,762.89	$348,519.57	$2,926,026.27	Weighted Total Sum of Extension
					$81,241.68	Conclusion of WTS divided by WTF
Weighted Percentage						
	Sale #1	Sale #2	Sale #3	Sale #4		
Sale Price	$85,000	$78,846	$79,257	$76,976		
Percentage of Weight	40%	20%	25%	15%	100% Contribution	
$ Contribution	$34,000.00	$15,769.20	$19,814.25	$11,546.40	$81,129.85	Sum of Contribution = Value

Chapter 4

Cost and Income Approaches Contribution to the Final Value

Chapter Objectives

- Conveyance of your Scope of Work Decision in Approaches to Value
- Communicating Components of the Cost Approach
- Recognize the Impact of the Income Approach to the Appraisal
- Techniques for Conveying Final Reconciliation and Comments for Clarity
- Clarifications on the pre-printed certification

Understanding the Steps of the Appraisal Process

The communication of the appraisal of a residential property most often is performed with a supplemented narrative to a form report. All too often appraisers take for granted the clients understand the appraisal process. An exhibit of the appraisal process is always a good idea for many clients. Steps 1-5 are the minimum points of the development.

Sample Commentary- "To understand the background of this Appraisal Report the Exhibit details the sequential steps of the Appraisal Process and Minimum Regulatory Steps in the Development and Reporting of This Market Value Conclusion."

Step 1

Definition of the Problem						
USPAP Assignment Elements of Scope of Work Rule				USPAP Standard Rule 1-2		
Identify client and other Intended Users	Identify the Intended Use	Identify the type and definition of Value	Identify the effective date	Identify relevant characteristics of the property	Assignment Conditions	
					Extraordinary Assumption	Hypothetical Conditions

Step 2

Scope of Work (Scope of Work Rule)
For each Appraisal assignment, an appraiser must complete three steps
1. Identify the problem to be solved (note steps above).
2. Determine and perform the scope of work necessary to develop credible assignment results; and
3. Disclose the scope of work in the report

Step 3

Data Collection and Analysis (Standard Rule 1-3)	
Market Analysis	**Highest and Best Use Analysis**
Demand Studies	Analyze the site "as if" or "as vacant"
Supply Duties	Analyze the site with the optimum improvement
Marketability Studies	Analyze the property "as it is currently improved"

Step 4		
Application of the Approaches to Value (Standard Rule 1-4)		
Cost	**Sales Comparison**	**Income Capitalization**
Develop an opinion of the Site Replicate a Cost to Build New Deduct the loss to the Cost New (Depreciation) Add Contribution of Site Improvements	Identify a criterion for selecting sales most similar to the subject. Deselect until the sales reflect the most similar alternative if the subject cannot be acquired. Adjust the sale prices for market recognized characteristics either inferior (add) or superior (subtract) to simulate a substitution. Reconcile from the adjusted sales a conclusion.	Develop an opinion of the Market Rent supported by comparable rental properties. Develop a capitalization rate from the local market area for the specific property type. Rental income deducted for expenses including vacancy is converted into a value by dividing the net operating income by a cap rate. Unadjusted gross rent converts into value through a multiplier (Value=Gross Scheduled Income x concluded multiplier)

Step 5
Reconciliation of Value Indicators into a Final Value (Standard Rule 1-6)
In developing a real property appraisal, an appraiser must:
(a) Reconcile the quality and quantity of data available and analyzed within the approaches used; and
(b) Reconcile the applicability and relevance of the approaches, methods and techniques used to arrive at the value conclusion(s)

Step 6
Reporting the Results of the Written Appraisal (Standard 2)
SR 2-1 Each written or oral real property appraisal report must: a) clearly and accurately set forth the appraisal in a manner that will not be misleading; b) contain sufficient information to enable the intended users of the appraisal to understand the report property; and c) clearly and accurately disclose all assumptions, extraordinary assumptions, hypothetical conditions, and limiting conditions used in the assignment.
SR 2-2 (a) Appraisal Report or (b) Restricted Appraisal Report
SR 2-3 Include a Signed Certification Statement (A statement of Ethical Obligations)

[1]To fully understand these summarized steps the intended users of this Appraisal Report should review the Uniform Standards of Professional Appraisal Practice (USPAP) which can be obtained from The Appraisal Foundation (www.appraisalfoundation.org).

The practicing appraiser must accept responsibility for ascertaining whether additional guidelines when the assignment calls for additional regulatory oversight. Appraisal assignments for mortgage lending that involves the intent to sell the loan to secondary markets binds the appraiser to additional communications and impacts their scope of work decisions as they are influenced by those secondary market directives. Those directives may conflict with the appraiser's belief on the what is necessary to develop a credible opinion of value. It is for that reason the Scope of Work Rule states, ***"An appraiser must not allow assignment conditions to limit the scope of work to such a degree that the assignment results are not credible in the context of the intended use."***

In an assignment that deals with Tax Dispute albeit federal or state, those laws governing those jurisdictions need to be reviewed for specific directives and/or formulas that may be applicable. In the cases of estate division or community property settlement, those laws in those jurisdictions need to be reviewed so that diligence in solving the appraisal problem is the ethical obligation of the appraiser who adheres to the best practice exhortations of the USPAP.

---

[1] The document known as USPAP also contains guidance to the document known as Advisory Opinions and Frequently Asked Questions as well as an Index to the document for specific subjects, illustrations of common misunderstandings and practical advice to questions asked by appraisers and other interested parties to valuation services. The steps shown in the exhibit are specific to real property appraisal. The document also offers best practice disciplines for real and personal property review, mass appraisal, personal property appraisal and business valuation.

4.1   Conveying Scope of Work Decisions

The Scope of Work decision making begins with recognizing the problem. The work order conveys the location, the property type, the type of assignment and the secondary market conditions, albeit Conventional, FHA, VA, etc. The pre-printed form directs what the secondary markets expect at a minimum.

> **SCOPE OF WORK:** The scope of work for this appraisal is defined by the complexity of this appraisal assignment and the reporting requirements of this appraisal report form, including the following definition of market value, statement of assumptions and limiting conditions, and certifications. The appraiser must, at a minimum: (1) perform a complete visual inspection of the interior and exterior areas of the subject property, (2) inspect the neighborhood, (3) inspect each of the comparable sales from at least the street, (4) research, verify, and analyze data from reliable public and/or private sources, and (5) report his or her analysis, opinions, and conclusions in this appraisal report.

This pre-printed statement opens with a general understanding, "The scope of work for this appraisal is ***defined by the complexity of this appraisal assignment*.....**" When the appraisal report is finished, there should be sufficient evidence to show the complexity of the assignment which may require a statement in the addendum.

Example: *Elaboration of the Scope of Work*-This assignment is defined as complex due to the minimal data sufficient to render, without additional critical reasoning, conclusions in every facet of the property specific analyses (market, site, improvement) and the appropriate approaches to value given the intended use and intended user. The intended use is for mortgage lending requiring this pre-printed form that has a methodology directive. Item #4 *"I developed my opinion of the market value of the real property that is the subject of this report based on the sales comparison approach to value. I have adequate comparable market data to develop a reliable sales comparison approach for this appraisal assignment. I further certify that I considered the cost and income approaches to value but did not develop them, unless otherwise indicated in this report."* The subject is an existing property in a rural market. That location limits the quantity of data with physical characteristics similar to the extent that adjustments were not necessary. Further, the dollar amount of the adjustments necessary to stabilize a comparison of the sale to the subject as an alternative substitute, is beyond the preferred close range. Those necessary adjustments are what the appraiser believes the market supports in its reaction to those differences. The Cost Approach was developed as the improvements were less than 5 years of actual age. It's reasonable to expect a buyer would similarly compare cost new to buying existing given the actual age. There is no indication an income production would be expected from the property therefore the Income Approach was deemed not necessary for credible results in the value. Although the sales were limited I believe they were sufficient to comply with the directive of this certification item."

> SR 2-2 (a)(vii) summarize the scope of work used to develop the appraisal; Comment: Because intended users' reliance on an appraisal may be affected by the scope of work, the report must enable them to be properly informed and not misled. Sufficient information includes disclosure of research and analyses performed and might also include disclosure of research and analyses not performed........"

This type of elaboration sets the stage for communicating the decisions made that involve performing analyses and approaches to value. It also serves as a means of compliance for supporting the elimination of any approach (required disclosure of [2]USPAP).

Do not limit your scope of work to the pre-printed boiler-plate on the form, especially when there is a level of difficulty. This insert shows the diligence of communicating the thought process the appraiser when through when going through the appraisal process.

4.2 Communicating the Cost Approach

Making the decision to develop the Cost Approach should be based on the need of the data and analyses results to contribute to the question of value. If the quantity and quality of the data is difficult to relate to replicating the improvements in their current condition. The last question to answer is whether the approach is appropriate. If through reasoning it can be concluded the approach will lend to the decision making about final value, that reasoning should be communicated in the body of the report.

Example: "The subject has been recently renovated with a total remodel of the kitchen and bathrooms in the past 3 years. The Cost Approach was believed to be relevant in that a prospective buyer could easily consider the value of buying the existing property in its current condition to building new and comparing the difference. Further, due to the recent renovation there was minimal physical depreciation. The market is stable to increasing indicating there is economic demand with no external obsolescence. Compared to sales similarly renovated there was no indication there was any super-adequacy or inadequacy. The minimal physical depreciation on the effective date, reasonably sufficient data for the development of site value, gave weight to this approach having relevance to the development of a credible indicator of value."

Documentation of the development of the cost new as well as the methodology for developing credibly the effective age and the economic life will define the strength of credible results for depreciation. Never communicate a qualified or quantified judgement without notation in the workfile as to how you came to that conclusion. If the depreciation reported was based on the age life method, the workfile must have evidence of how both the effective age and economic life were determined.

> *Never communicate a qualified or quantified judgement without notation in the workfile as to how you came to that*

---

[2] The inset is not the complete SR in SR 2-2(a)(vii). For a complete understanding refer to the 2016-2017 USPAP.

4.3   Communication of the Income Approach in a Residential Appraisal

One-to-Four Units or single unit condominiums, townhouses and detached single family have the functional capability for being used as rental property. Often appraisers will take the work order literally when they develop their appraisals and will report, "The Income Approach was not requested in this assignment." This becomes a questionable scope of work decision when the work order also says, "Refinance of Tenant Occupied Property". The Scope of Work decision is made considerate of communication with the client but, it is not the client who bears the responsibility or accountability for the appraiser's Scope of Work decision. That burden belongs to the appraiser.

In general, the requested forms that involve residential income production will typically be:
- 1025   2-4 Unit Residential Appraisal Form
- 1007   Market Rent form
- 216   Operating Income Statement
- 1004   Single Family with the attachments of form 216 and 1007

Capitalization Rates and Multipliers are the mathematical factors that convert the income into a value. Even though the forms communicate some of the work and the results of the application of the factors to the net or gross incomes, the appraiser should develop minimum directives of communication when the Income Approach is part of the appraisal assignment. For clarity of understanding the appraiser's scope of work that involves the development of the Income Approach, the report should contain narrative commentary summarizing:
- Why the Income Approach was found necessary in the Scope of Work plan to solve the appraisal problem
- How the expenses (when expenses are a component of the rate or multiplier) were determined
- The weight of the Income Approach in the final value conclusion

The problem appraisers wrestle with is the directive of item #4 in the pre-printed certification form(s) discussed earlier.

Item #4 in the 1004 certification statement says, " "*I developed my opinion of the market value of the real property that is the subject of this report based on the sales comparison approach to value. I have adequate comparable market data to develop a reliable sales comparison approach for this appraisal assignment. I further certify that I considered the cost and income approaches to value but did not develop them, unless otherwise indicated in this report.*"

Notice, the last sentence doesn't say you must not develop the Income or Cost Approaches, it says you did consider the additional methodologies. It states the cost and income approaches were considered and not developed, unless otherwise indicated. That "otherwise indicated" is the springboard back to the appraiser's responsibility for making the appropriate Scope of Work decision. An approach to value development is dependent on:

- Quantity of Data
- Quality of the Data
- Appropriateness of the Approach and is driven also by,
- Intended User and Intended Use of the Appraisal

Sample Comment: "The intended use of the Appraisal Report was for a mortgage loan decision of a tenant occupied property. The property owner acquired this real property asset for its income production benefit. In this bounded neighborhood, the appraiser has found comparable rental properties. There were however, no sales of tenant occupied properties. The Gross Rent Multiplier (GRM) reported was extrapolated by considering the comparable sales ability to generate a market rent. The research and conclusions of market rent was imposed under a hypothetical condition to the comparable sales in order to extrapolate what the GRM would be if the sales were tenant occupied at the time of their sale. That specific assumption of economic opportunity, not exercised on the effective date of this appraisal, produced a range of GRM's that were reconciled as reported on the form. The use of this condition, known to be false, could affect the appraisal analysis and findings in the Income Approach. For this reason, a margin of error naturally exists within this specific approach and its indicator of value. Details of the research and resulting calculations of various multipliers can be found in the workfile of this appraisal."

4.4   Making the Final Value Decision

Daily practicing appraisers are challenged with concluding a value and more often than not, a single point of value. It's important to be reminded of two specific definitions (set forth in the USPAP document).

- *APPRAISAL: (noun) the act or process of developing an opinion of value; an opinion of value. (adjective) of or pertaining to appraising and related functions such as appraisal practice or appraisal services.*

Comment: *An appraisal must be numerically expressed as a specific amount, as a range of numbers, or as a relationship (e.g., not more than, not less than) to a previous value opinion or numerical benchmark (e.g., assessed value, collateral value).*

- *VALUE: the monetary relationship between properties and those who buy, sell, or use those properties.*

Comment: *Value expresses an economic concept. As such, it is never a fact but always an opinion of the worth of a property at a given time in accordance with a specific definition of value. In appraisal practice, value must always be qualified - for example, market value, liquidation value, or investment value.*

Notice that the word "appraisal" pertains to or is an act or process of developing an opinion which is the WHY in the expression of the result being communicated as:
1. A specific amount, or
2. As a range of numbers, or
3. As a relationship to a previous value or numerical benchmark

Whereas the word "value" is an economic concept of a worth that MUST BE ALWAYS qualified. The examples of how that economic concept is qualified is by stating the type of the value, albeit Market Value, Liquidation Value, or Investment Value.
Recognizing the differences between these two words and the commentary on the need to qualify the opinion by the definitions alone prompt the need for writing a summary of how the opinion was concluded.
Some appraisers will use weighted techniques to document their critical reasoning process. In chapter 3 (page 3-26) there were examples of weighted techniques that are useful in the Sales Approach. In the final value step, the USPAP requires communication sufficient for the client and intended users to understand the appraiser's reasoning.
Note the directive of SR 2-2 (a) (viii) and within the comment the emphasis on communicating on the results of the development of the final value.

[3]2-2 (a) (viii) *summarize the information analyzed, the appraisal methods and techniques employed, and the reasoning that supports the analyses, opinions, and conclusions; exclusion of the sales comparison approach, cost approach, or income approach must be explained;*

*Comment: An Appraisal Report must include sufficient information to indicate that the appraiser complied with the requirements of STANDARD 1. The amount of detail required will vary with the significance of the information to the appraisal. The appraiser must provide sufficient information to enable the client and intended users to understand the rationale for the opinions and conclusions, **including reconciliation of the data and approaches, in accordance with Standards Rule 1-6**.*

When reporting an opinion of market value, a summary of the results of analyzing the subject sales, agreements of sale, options, and listings in accordance with Standards Rule 1-5 is required. If such information is unobtainable, a statement on the efforts undertaken by the appraiser to obtain the information is required. If such information is irrelevant, a statement acknowledging the existence of the information and citing its lack of relevance is required.

There is another weighted analysis that can be used to assist in the decision for a final value when more than one approach to value is used.

Weighted Technique for Final Reconciliation	Scale 1-5 1= Low, 5 = High Points			
Standard Rule 1-6				
	Cost	Sales	Income	Combined Total
Quantity of Data	3	3	0	6
Quality of Data	3	3	0	6
Appropriateness of the Approach	2	5	0	7
Total Points	8	11	0	19
÷ Combined Total	19	19		
= % of Contribution of Each Approach	0.42105263	0.578947368		
Indicated Value	$914,487	$900,000		
X Weight of the Approach to Value	0.42105263	0.578947368		
$'s Contribution to Final Value	$385,047	$521,053		
Sum of Contribution	**$906,100**			

The grid shown is not normally found in the residential appraisal report, its information that is in the workfile. What the appraiser must do, to be in compliance with USPAP, is to convey how they reasoned the value.

---

[3] Excerpt from the 2016-2017 USPAP. For complete understanding including additional guidance through advisory opinions and FAQs go to www.appraisalfoundation.org for a copy of the current USPAP

Sample Comment:
In the final conclusion of value for this market value decision, the appraiser recognized the client and intended users were most interested in the sales of similar property types. The adjusted conclusions of the Sales Approach were Sale #1 $908,000, Sale #2 $905,500, Sale #3 $910,000. The Sales Contract had an accepted offer of $906,000 which was within the range of the adjusted sales. Because the property has been recently remodeled over the past 2 years a Cost Approach was contributory in its indicator of value. The Cost Approach concluded a value of $911,000 which was near in its conclusion value to that of adjusted Sale #3. The appraiser believed Sale #2 was the most similar, requiring the least number of adjustments as well as the least dollars of net and gross percent. Weighting the quantity of data, quality of data and appropriateness of the approach a technique of weighting was developed with a conclusion of $905,500. This conclusion was also in close agreement with the adjusted value of Sale #2 and the pending contract which represents an agreement between a knowledgeable buyer and seller. For these reasons, the appraiser has concluded the current market value is $906,000.

4.5   The Certification Statement

The appraiser has both a competency obligation when developing their value opinion as well as an ethical obligation when reporting their conclusion of value. The pre-printed form has _**twenty-five**_ certifications whereas the USPAP has only _**ten**_ Ethical Obligations required to be stated. The difference is due to the Secondary Markets, who developed the appraisal forms for Mortgage Lending. Those underwriting Intended Users have certain risks they've identified that are lessened when there are limitations to the development of the opinion. The additions of the fifteen certification statements (which does not include the History of Service obligation of USPAP that must be also stated in the certification) are not ethical directives, they are mechanical. For example, nowhere in the USPAP Statement of Certification, will you find an obligation to only include information you derived from disinterested sources. In fact, that obligation goes beyond the possible. Yet certification statement #10 states, "I verified, from a disinterested source, all information in this report that was provided by parties who have a financial interest in the sale or financing of the subject property."

You will not find in the USPAP statement of certification, "I researched, verified, analyzed, and reported on any offering for sale of the subject property in the twelve months prior to the effective date of this appraisal." Under SR 1-5 the requirement for development is, "[4]analyze all agreements of sale, options, and listings of the subject property current as of the effective date of the appraisal; and..." The secondary market put a time limit of 12 months. Further, the pre-printed form threatens the appraiser by stating no certification statement can be removed nor can it depart from the intent of the items on the form. This prompts a written narrative commentary and a clarification on the items noted on the form that are not USPAP specific, ethical directives.

---

[4] Excerpt from 2016-2017 edition of USPAP, specific language comes from SR 1-5(a)

Sample Comment:
Certification Statement Subsection
"The intended user is informed that these statements represent the ethical obligations of the appraiser. These statements are pre-printed; *clarifications* are necessary so the intended users are not misled as to the limitations of these statements. Under the appraiser's obligatory development and communication expectations of competency, the intended user has a right to understand the information sufficiently to such an extent that decisions, which prompted the appraisal order, can be made. For this reason, certain clarifications are presented."

Clarifications are recommended to be made for pre-printed certification numbers:
2, 5, 7, 10, 14, 17, 19, 21, 23 and the additional required disclosure of certification about the history of service if the software being used does not have this certification built into the form.

Certification Additional Item 26: "In accordance with the current USPAP edition the requirement of work history over a three-year period must be disclosed prior to acceptance of the assignment (or if discovered after acceptance during the research in the assignment). The appraiser disclosed at the time of the assignment they had historically appraised,_____,_____ the subject of the assignment <u>two and one-half (note date you had historical activity)</u>_____ years ago. The client is a <u>financial institution (identify by type)</u>_who engaged the appraiser by their agent, an AMC known as (name)_____ and was informed at the time of the assignment the appraiser's history of real estate activity. The client did not reject the appraiser being awarded this assignment. The appraiser acknowledges this history, the disclosure to the client of that historical activity with the property to be appraised and certifies they do not believe this history impugns the ability of this appraiser to perform the assignment in an objective, independent and impartial competent manner."

Or when no history exists (note the following page)

Certification Additional Item 26: "In accordance the 2012-2013 USPAP edition the requirement of work history over a three-year period must be disclosed prior to acceptance of the assignment (or if discovered after acceptance during the research in the assignment). The appraiser makes it known they *did not* perform any service as an appraiser or in any other capacity, regarding the property that is the subject of this report within the three-year period immediately preceding acceptance of this assignment. "

4.6   Periodic Review of the Appraisal Report

There can be no better time spent than to periodically review your own appraisal report. If there is sufficient manpower within the office it is recommended they be given a copy of the report and a short checklist that ensures commentary necessary due to USPAP, Secondary Market Requirements and Client Overlays (specific policies of the Lender) are located within the report. Some appraisers have organized templates that house all of those additions by having capitalized headers which prompt the appraiser to communicate in those specific areas.

Example:
- Market Value Definition Source
- History of Service
- Value difference from Pending Price
- Market Value conclusion greater than or less than the predominant price
- Contract Analysis
- Exclusions of Approaches to Value
- Highest and Best Use support for stated conclusion
- Support for the reported site value, effective age, economic life

The list above is not all inclusive, a good place to start when developing a checklist is with Standard Rule 2, then adapt and expand as needed based on the secondary market's needs (or other mandatory additions for private transactions based on jurisdictional legal requirements).

Chapter 5

Solution Chapter

Chapter Objectives

- Review exercises and case studies with recommended solutions
- Enhance participant's skills through affirmation of solved problems

Exercise 1
What are three things you learned from the "boilerplate" example?

Below are greater than three items; any one of the three would be a contributive statement adding to the understanding of the location

1. Subject is in a Rural Location
2. Lack of proximity to major shopping centers and public transportation is not an adverse factor
3. Distance to urban location is less than 30 minutes' drive
4. Location of nearest urban area is less than 40 miles
5. Appeal for Rural Markets is lax governmental regulations and quiet enjoyment

1.3 Discussion Question(s)

1. Why is the contract pending relevant to the appraisal assignment?
    i.   Shows agreement between two parties on an available property
    ii.   May show a market reaction to a difference
    iii.   Indicates a price willing to be accepted by a seller for a specific property in a location
2. Why is the history of the past three years relevant to the appraisal assignment?
    i.   Can show a change in the market reaction
    ii.   Can indicate a change to the subject property (vacant land to improved land)
    iii.   May support a market trend

1.3.1 Discussion Question(s):

1. The first Question is did you analyze the contract. [x] or
2. If you did not analyze the contract explain why.   [x]

Notice there are three directives of communication:

1. There must be a summary of the results of analyzing the SUBJECT sales, agreements of sale, options, and listings in accordance with SR 1-5, and
2. If such information is unobtainable, a statement on the efforts undertaken by the appraiser to obtain the information is required.
3. If such information is irrelevant, a statement acknowledging the existence of the information and citing its lack of relevance is required.

1.3.3.1 Practice Exercise

Based on the preceding page (1-14):

1. What is the dominant transaction type (dominant type of financing)?

   _____Conventional_____

2. Is there a trend that can be identified on concessions?

   ___Dominance of Seller Paid with range 4.5-6%_____

3. Is it customary for personal property to pass with the sale?

   _____Yes_____

1.3.3.2 Solution to Writing Exercise

(NOTE: THIS IS A SAMPLE ONLY) Twenty sales were initially researched to study the behavior of the sales in the subject's market area. Five transactions of the 20 were selected for the final most suitable comparison. The questions asked of the data collected were 1) dominance of financing, 2) dominance of seller paid concessions, 3) dominance of personal property given by seller to buyer included in the sale price, 4) Days on the Market between offering date and contract closed date, 5) the percent of list to sale ratio. Each factor of the contract was reviewed and compared. The conclusions were that Conventional terms are the dominant financing arrangements, with reported Loan to Value ratios from 80%-100%. The subject is seeking an 80% loan. The sale to list price ratio is in keeping with the market median of 97%, median dollars of concessions were $11,700, median percent of concession was 4.5%. The subject's contract was within 10% of the median price, and the concession 4.8% were near the market median. The conclusion is this contract is performing in the bounds of central tendency based on similar comparable sales.

Solution to Chapter 2

— Write the characteristics that match the influences and sources of where you could obtain that information? An example is offered for each to assist your thought process.

Factor	Neighborhood Characteristic	Source
Demand	Ratio of # Listings to # Sales	MLS
	DAYS ON MARKET <30	MLS, Local Realtors, Appraiser Files
Scarcity	Percentage of Built Up	Aerial Map
	Specific plan limiting number of lots in a specific location or limited physical characteristic such as waterfront property	Master Plan, Builder, Agents, Pictures, Plat Maps
Utility	Proximity to Employment	City Data
	Demographics (is there a need for 2 or 3 bedroom, 2 or > bathroom)	Census Data
	Surrounding Improvements	MLS, Real Estate Agents,
Transferability	Financing Availability	Comparable Sales
	Special Loan Programs	Local Lenders
	Owner Finance	Contract
	Assumptions	RE Agents
	Favorable Interest Rates	Local Lenders

2.2.2 Case Study – Using the partial sentences that convey communicating some of the key elements relevant to a residential neighborhood, finish the comment.
Demand

1. The ratio of comparable listings to comparable sales is 8:1; the typical ratio of listings-to-sales is 3:1. The abundance of competing listings creates an oversupply which will impact the days on the market and number of months of housing supply.

1. The days on the market trend fluctuation is based on the season surrounding the effective date. The effective date of this appraisal is 5/25/2017, the demand for housing on this effective date month enters the season of high demand. This fact positively affects the forecasted days on the market. It was this seasonal influence that impacted the projected marketing time in the neighborhood section of the Appraisal Report.

Scarcity

1. The subdivision where the subject is located has favorable views of the natural lake with 20 lots left that actually front the water. The view of the lake extends to the houses on first and second row from the water. This feature has a positive impact on the demand for the location, projected to continue for an indeterminant future.

2. There are only two High Rise Condominium Projects in the bounded neighborhood. Over the past 12 months 2 bedroom units sell within 90 days of being listed with no concessions once placed on the market. The demand for the units is related to the lack of availability.

Solution to 2.3.1 Case Study Exercise
Looking at the chart to the right, identify the largest
number of households.

$75,000 - $99,000

1.3.2   Solution to Case Study Exercise
Using a multiplier of 3 indicate the predominant
price these households could afford in this zip code.

$ _225,000_ - $ _297,000_ = Predominant Range

1.3.3   Solution to Case Study Exercise
Write a brief narrative that explains the segments of
the markets and what the subject's conclusion of
$650,000 represents, including a response to the
distance the subject's concluded market value is
from the predominant price calculated in the
preceding Case Study Exercise (2.3.2).

Zip Code 78201 Household Income	
Income (Yr. 2015)	#Households
Less than $10,000	729
$10,000 to $14,999	1,482
$15,000 to $19,999	1,124
$20,000 to $24,999	1,143
$25,000 to $29,999	1,148
$30,000 to $34,999	843
$35,000 to $39,999	937
$40,000 to $45,999	636
$50,000 to $59,999	1,241
$60,000 to $74,999	1,128
$75,000 to $99,000	1,556
$100,000 to $124,999	596
$125,000 to $149,999	299
$150,000 to $199,999	251
$200,000 or more	120

*The pool of qualified buyers is limited in this demographic area for this property and its
concluded value. The subject is not overbuilt and is within the affordability range of this income
level reported by the census.*

2.4.1 Case Study Exercise: Is there a connect or a disconnect between the comments in
the site section and the addendum on the form? Explain: Yes, sites in this area appear to
be 2+ acres, the fact the subject has 55+ acres indicates there may be excess land which
should be discussed in the body of the report and in the Highest and Best Use
addendum.

2.4.2 Case Study Exercise
Based on the information presented does the highest and best use commentary convey
understanding and support for the rationale of the highest and best use conclusion? No

What additional understanding do you think should be addressed in this subject highest and best use?
The subject is complex due to its location and its size of parcel. There should be an in-depth discussion
about whether or not the land was considered Excess or Surplus and if divisible (being Excess), was there
a market demand for the division. The view of woods and access to the lake and potential for building a
dock would be a consideration that should have been detailed to ensure the conclusion of highest and
best use was credibly developed.

Solution to Chapter 3

Exercise: Circle which of the examples below shows compliance with UAD requirements?

Data Source(s)		Austin MLS #7010219;DOM 143	Austin MLS #4793298;DOM 83	Austin MLS #2180506;DOM 59
Verification Source(s)		CAD-Keller Williams Realty	CAD-RE/Max	CAD-Keller Williams Realty

Data Source(s)		MLS 102367;DOM 221	MLS 102239;DOM 146	MLS 102314;DOM 125
Verification Source(s)		UCAD	UCAD	UCAD

Data Source(s)		SABOR MLS #886179;DOM 184	SABOR MLS #911252;DOM 74	Settlement Statement;DOM Unk
Verification Source(s)		Tax Record	Tax Record	Tax Record

3.4.1 Solution to *Exercise:* What's wrong with the UAD communication of the grid?

Answer: ___Comma in the site area needs to be removed___

VALUE ADJUSTMENTS	DESCRIPTION	DESCRIPTION	+(-) $ Adjustment	DESCRIPTION	+(-) $ Adjustment	DESCRIPTION	+(-) $ Adjustment
Sales or Financing		ArmLth		ArmLth		ArmLth	
Concessions		VA;0	0	Conv;0	0	VA;0	0
Date of Sale/Time		s10/11;c08/11	0	s03/12;c02/12	0	s04/12;c02/12	0
Location	N;Res;	N;Res;		N;Res;		N;Res;	
Leasehold/Fee Simple	Fee Simple	Fee Simple		Fee Simple		Fee Simple	
Site	1.23 ac	21,344 sf	7500	24,394 sf	7500	21,344 sf	7500
View	N;Res;	N;Res;		N;Res;		N;Res;	
Design (Style)	Ranch	Ranch		Contemporary	0	Mediterranean	0
Quality of Construction	Q2	Q2		Q3	12000	Q3	12000
Actual Age	0	0		6	6000	7	7000
Condition	C1	C1		C2	0	C2	0
Above Grade	Total / Bdrms. / Baths	Total / Bdrms. / Baths		Total / Bdrms. / Baths		Total / Bdrms. / Baths	
Room Count	11 / 4 / 3.1	11 / 5 / 4.1	-5000	10 / 4 / 4.0	-3500	9 / 4 / 3.1	0
Gross Living Area	4339 sq.ft.	4499 sq.ft.	-10400	4277 sq.ft.	4030	3971 sq.ft.	23920

1. Based on the information reported in Exhibits 4.2 and 4.3, is there consistency between the analysis of the 1004MC and the One-Unit Housing Trends? _____ Yes __X__ No

2. What comments would be appropriate given the observation of the One-Unit Housing Trend and the 1004MC?

    The answers provided are the basic responses. More discussion may arise as a consequence of the exercise. "There is clearly a large reduction in the number of sales which shows a seller reaction that has pulled back their offerings. It's possible the columns represent too few transactions to offer quantified analysis for the conclusions of the Neighborhood. The report needs to detail why there is a different conclusion from that of the 1004MC."

Made in the USA
Columbia, SC
10 June 2021